Hans Christian Andersen's COPENHAGEN

A fairy tale walk through the City

Text: Bente Kjølbye   Photos: Ole Larsen

Høst & Søns Forlag · København

1992

The book is translated into English by Ian Cocker
Layout by Erik Ellegaard Frederiksen
Typeset by Tommy Rasmussen Sats ApS, Køge
Reproduction by Lindholm Repro A/S, Herlev
Printed in Denmark by A-Offset, Holstebro 1992

ISBN 87-14-29123-1

The publication is supported by
Augustinus Fonden
Carlsbergs Mindelegat for J.C.Jacobsen
Hafnia Fonden
Konsul George Jorck og Hustru Emma Jorck's Fond
Marie & M.B. Richters Fond

This book is the outcome of fruitful and inspiring collaboration between the author and the photographer instigated by Ole Larsen.

There is both a demonic and a romantic element in this portrait of Hans Christian Andersen by August Grahl (1846). His longish hair and his elegantly-tied cravat are reminiscent of other artistic European contemporaries such as Chopin and Liszt. Beneath the surface, however, he is Danish. On the left in the picture he has written in German, “Life is full of sunshine and the best always happens.”

The Poetic Copenhagen

This book takes us on a guided walk through Copenhagen from Frederiksberg Hill to Amalienborg Palace, from Nyhavn to The Little Mermaid. The route we shall take traces the footsteps of Hans Christian Andersen through the streets of Copenhagen during the 56 years that he lived here – from 1819 to 1875. It must be said, however, that the Poet was a restless soul with no place to call home – a nomad who loved to travel and who loved to move on. Often he would be gone for months at a time on his journeys through Europe. Back in Denmark, he liked to stay at a hotel – it felt as if he was on his travels again – and throughout his entire life he owned neither a house nor an apartment. It was not until nine years before his death that he acquired his own bed. The bed now stands in the Hans Christian Andersen Museum in Odense. A shudder ran through the Danish people when, after the completion of his Hans Christian Andersen film, Danny Kaye actually had the temerity to lie on this holy of holies.

Hans Christian Andersen himself would probably have regarded the incident with equanimity, for he never cared to be bound by material things. When he died, he was homeless. Just one month earlier he had given notice at No.18, Nyhavn.

Hans Christian Andersen's works are as topical as ever, and his strange life is still constantly subjected to new interpretations. Why this poor shoemaker's son was blessed with literary talents no-one can say. His early schooling was meagre. He was never together with other children, but spent his time playing with toy theatres and puppets. He was an oddity. His spiritual sustenance consisted of the books he read and the prophesies of wise women, who foretold a brilliant future for him.

Later on he loved to talk about his life and he wrote a number of autobiographies. «Levnedsbogen« ("Autobiography") depicts his life up until his 28th year. "The Fairy Tale of My Life" is a more literary work describing his fairy-tale path from poverty to world-wide fame.

It was only when he was 17 years old that he was offered a proper school education – but then with no financial worries attached! He thus became a schoolboy at Slagelse Grammar School, where learning grammar, mathematics, and Latin by rote were the order of the day – although Andersen would much rather have been writing stories. This period is marked by Headmaster Meisling's lack of understanding and the many insults he heaped upon the young Andersen when the imagination of this sensitive spirit ran away with him.

For this dreamer and creator of visions it was a blessed relief to complete his studies and leave Slagelse Grammar School. He now possessed the tools of learning and was at last permitted to write, to become himself! In "The Fairy Tale of My Life" he writes of his imagination: "The angels had planted the seed there while I still lay slumbering in my cradle. The seed grew, it spread its magic fragrance, Imagination, and this wonderful flower of life unfolded more and more within my heart."

The Poet was always at work, even when he didn't actually have a pen in his hand. Everything he experienced was turned into novels and accounts of his journeys, into fairy tales and stories. His life, beginning in total obscurity and ending in world-wide acclaim, was a fairy tale in itself.

Hans Christian Andersen's importance is beyond measure – to such an extent have his words and thoughts entered into the Danish consciousness as something completely natural. Not a day goes by without his name being mentioned in one context or another. He is quoted with equal frequency by the literati, sports journalists, and advertising people alike. It is simply impossible to imagine Denmark without Hans Christian Andersen.

We need him every bit as much as did his contemporaries. Who, for example, has no need of the goodness, the compassion, which makes "Thumbelina" kiss the frozen swallow's eyes?

In Hans Christian Andersen's fairy tales, however, good and evil are by no means absolutes. The birds also sing for the wicked. The sensitive Poet knew from experience what an uplifting effect acts of compassion have on people and, conversely, how easy it is to hurt people and make them insecure.

Hopefully, this book will make you want to go in search of Hans Christian Andersen in Copenhagen. It will take you to his many different addresses and tell you of his circle of friends and acquaintances in the capital.

The themes of the illustrations are taken from the Poet's life and fairy tales. Inspired by his imagery, we will try to create an impression of that intimate Copenhagen which still flourishes today. The poet in the story of "Auntie Toothache" sees the town in his own original way, "Often, as I walk through the streets of the town, it seems to me as if I am walking through a large library: the houses are like bookcases, each floor is a shelf of books. There you can see a story from our everyday life, there is a good old comedy, scientific works on every possible subject, over here smut and good reading. I can dream and philosophize on all the literature that surrounds me."

So now you have the chance to be a Real Poet! With this book as your guide, visit the places Hans Christian Andersen lived in and frequented. Use your eyes and your imagination. Look around you and find the poetic Copenhagen – both as it was in the Poet's time and as it still is today.

Flights of Fantasy in the King's Garden

Before we start our walk, we must imagine that we are sitting, invisible, on a bench in Kongens Have – "The King's Garden" (entrance from Gothersgade, see map).

Behold, beside us on the bench, the aspiring poet – a young boy of 14, poor as a church mouse, infinitely gangling and bony. His eyes are small as peas, his nose protrudes much too far from his pale face. He huddles up in his thin clothes to keep warm and to keep his hunger at bay. His meal is nothing but a little piece of wheat bread. His landlady in Dybensgade thinks that he has his meals with some family or other in town, so she has given him nothing but a cup of coffee for breakfast. Anyway, he couldn't afford to pay her for anything more than his lodgings.

He sits there wondering what is to become of him when his eyes come to rest on Rosenborg, the old copper-clad palace by the moat. What magnificence and splendour there must be inside! All his misery and hardships are forgotten and he sees before him a real princess. Drenched by the rain and the foul weather, she knocks at the gate. The old king in person comes to open up – clad in dressing gown, nightcap, and carpet slippers. He does not yet know that she is a real princess. But that is what she is. Soon she will sleep on 20 eiderdown mattresses and 20 featherbeds, and still feel the little pea through all the thick layers. So in credible is the whole story that the pea is taken to the Royal Cabinet of Curiosities, where it is put on exhibition for all to see.

The young boy takes a bite of his bread and, as courting couples pass by, new images appear to his mind's eye. He sees a chubby and naked little boy whose name is Cupid, who is armed with bow and arrow and who possesses an awesome power: "When the students are returning from their lectures and the young girls coming back from

Kongens Have has not changed much since Hans Christian Andersen's days. Find a bench and – like the Poet – sit here for a while. It was here that Andersen found his inspiration for *The Tinder-Box*.

church, he pierces their breast with his darts." Cupid is love embodied. Not even old people will he leave in peace. A poet who has given him shelter he shoots "straight through the heart so that the old Poet lay on the floor weeping".

That is "The Naughty Boy" who runs around in Kongens Have and on the ramparts of the town.

Up at the palace the soldiers march back and forth on sentry duty – left, right! left, right! – and the young boy's imagination runs away with him again. "A soldier came marching along the highroad – left, right! left right!" Over there by the hollow tree stands the witch. She knows that beneath the tree there are long passages with treasure chests – it is just that she can't get down there herself. But as soon as she sets eyes on the soldier, the story of the Tinder-Box is under way. The fierce lions which guard the wrought iron gate to the palace in the garden are transformed by imagination into three big dogs. The largest of them has eyes each as big as the Round Tower, "And they rolled round and round like wheels." From Kongens Have it was easy to see just how big the Round Tower was because, in Andersen's time, it literally towered above all the houses in Copenhagen.

The lions in front of *Rosenborg* provided Andersen with the inspiration for the three fierce dogs in *The Tinder-Box*.

But the soldier shares the Poet's zest for life. He lifts the dogs down and when he sees the gold, his eyes too become large and round. "Heavens! What a lot of gold there was! He could buy the whole of Copenhagen, and all the sugar-pigs from the cake women, all the tin soldiers, whips, and rocking horses in the world. Yes, that was money indeed!"

And now life became a bed of roses: "Now he led a very merry life. He went to the theatre, drove through the King's Garden and gave away lots and lots of money to the poor, which was nice of him! He knew from past experience how miserable it was not to have a penny in your pocket."

Hans Christian Andersen never forgot who and what he had been at the start – even though he ended up having everything that he had ever dreamed of.

The Poet is always present in his fairy tales. As an actor he appears in many disguises, a master of transformation. In "The Ugly Duckling" he is the duckling which turns into a beautiful swan. In "The Shadow" he is the man who succumbs to the power of his own shadow. In "The Snail and The Rose Bush" he is the rose bush which just stands there blooming. He is also the Little Mermaid whose love carries her into immortality.

Everything that the Poet sees and experiences inspires him – including Copenhagen. And this is where our walk starts – at the very spot where the Poet's own fairy tale started – on Frederiksberg Hill.

Rosenborg was built as a summer palace by Christian IV in the 17th Century. Christian IV himself decided how the palace should look and he loved to live here. The palace was also the royal treasury. The crown regalia and the crown jewels were kept here and money was stored in the cellars. A brave soldier might just be able to get at these riches through a hollow tree! At any rate it was a mirage for a poor boy who sat there every day gnawing at a stale crust.

On Frederiksberg Hill

On 6th September, 1819, a boy climbed down from the stagecoach from Odense. There he stood on Frederiksberg Bakke – "Frederiksberg Hill" – clutching his small bundle. From the hill he could see right as far as Vesterport and, beyond, the church spires rising up. He had said goodbye to the town of his birth to seek fame and fortune in Copenhagen. Now, having got so close to the object of his yearning, he burst into tears. He realised how utterly alone he was. The Good Lord in Heaven was his only support.

"The Boy Hans Christian Andersen" it said in his travel permit, which was required at that time. His worldly fortune consisted of just ten rixdollars. Nevertheless he firmly believed that he would get on in the world.

At that time Frederiksberg lay far outside the city, which only really started at Vesterport – where the city gate stood. How simple and rural Frederiksberg then was Andersen describes in the story of "The Key to the Gate".

"It was in the time of King Frederik the Sixth. Copenhagen in those days had no gas lighting – it had train oil lamps instead. It had no Tivoli and no Casino Theatre. No trams and no railways. There were few entertainments compared to what we have now. On Sunday people would walk from the Gate to the Assistens Cemetery, read the inscriptions on the graves, sit on the grass, eat their picnic lunch and drink their "snaps" (aquavit). Or they would go to Frederiksberg, where there was a regimental band in front of the palace and crowds of people to see the Royal Family rowing past on the narrow canals with the old King at the helm. He and the Queen would greet everyone without regard to differences of rank or station. Well-to-do families would come out here from the town to drink their evening tea. They could get hot water at the little farmhouse in the field outside the park, but they had to bring their own tea urn."

The day the fourteen-year-old Hans Christian Ander-

In Hans Christian Andersen's time the respectable classes would go on Sunday outings to *Frederiksberg Have* (Frederiksberg Garden), particularly to enjoy the sight of Frederik VI and the beloved royal family, with the King himself at the tiller, being rowed around the canals.

In 1819, from the top of the hill, just next to *Frederiksberg Palace*, the 14-year-old Hans Christian Andersen looked out across Copenhagen for the first time. In those days the palace lay outside the city. It was built in 1699 by Frederik IV. Between 1794 and 1801, the original French garden was turned into a park on the lines of English landscape gardens. Now as then the garden provides a pleasant setting for people to enjoy themselves.

Bakkehuset, now a museum, is associated first and foremost with Kamma and Knud Lyhne Rahbek. These two people gathered around them a large and happy circle of friends, including most of the writers of the time. The young Hans Christian Andersen was a regular visitor here. Kamma was the first person to call him "poet", and for this he was always to remember her.

sen arrived in Copenhagen he regarded as his second birthday – and he celebrated it wherever in the world he might be. It was also in Frederiksberg – at Bakkehuset – that he was called a poet for the first time – and, furthermore, by one of the great literary ladies of that period, Kamma Rahbek.

In "The Fairy Tale of My Life" he tells how, "The widow of Denmark's famous statesman, Christian Colbjørnsen, and her daughter were the first two people of the upper classes to give the poor boy that I was a kind reception. Mrs Colbjørnsen used to spend the summer at Bakkehuset ("Hill House"), which was owned by Rahbek, the poet, and his wife. Rahbek himself never spoke to me. Mrs Rahbek, on the other hand, with her vivacity and her friendly nature, talked with me a good deal. I had started to write a kind of comedy and read it aloud to her. After the first few scenes she exclaimed: 'But there are whole passages in it you have copied out of Oehlenschlæger and Ingemann!' – Yes, but they are so beautiful, I replied in all innocence, and continued reading. One day, as I was on my way up from her to Mrs Colbjørnsen, she handed me a bunch of roses and said: 'Will you take them up to her? I am sure it would please the Privy Councillor's Widow to receive them from the hand of a poet!' These words were spoken partly in fun, but it was the first time anyone had mentioned my name in connexion with the word 'poet'. It seared through my body and soul. Tears came to my eyes and I know that, from this moment on, my mind was made up to become a writer and poet. Up until then it had only been a game as a change from the puppet theatre. Now it was something higher – now it was the goal!"

Today Bakkehuset is a museum. The Rahbeks' home is preserved as it was during the Danish Golden Age period, with candles lit in the various rooms when visitors come to look around. Here too you can buy a postcard of Hans Christian Andersen from a painting by E.Jerichau Baumann – although the poet Andersen was by no means a main figure in the home at that time, merely one of the many who enjoyed Kamma Rahbek's hospitality.

The address of the museum, "Bakkehusmuseet", is Rahbeks Allé 23. The museum is open 11.00-15.00 on Wednesdays, Thursdays, and Saturdays, as well as Sundays and public holidays throughout the year. Walk down Frederiksberg Hill (Roskildevej), turn right into Pile Allé and shortly after you will see a sign pointing left to Rahbeks Allé and Bakkehuset, which you will find just near the corner on the right.

The King of Entertainment and the Chinese Emperor

Our route through Copenhagen proper starts at Rådhuspladsen – The Town Hall Square – by the statue of Hans Christian Andersen. Completed in 1969, the statue is the work of sculptor Henry Luchow-Nielsen. Behind us are H.C.Andersens Boulevard and Tivoli, which did not exist when the young Andersen came to town. It was the entrepreneur Georg Carstensen who, in 1843, was granted permission to establish a pleasure garden on the old ramparts outside Vesterport. The lake in Tivoli is actually part of the old moat around the town.

Right from the start Tivoli had everything which Copenhageners know and love to this day: music, pantomimes, artistes, festivals, illuminations, and fireworks. In those days, incidentally, the fireworks were lit by no less a personage than Major War Commissioner Høeg-Guldberg.

The Chinese Bazaar was one of Tivoli's most beautiful buildings, a pavilion with slender columns and painted in light colours. It was so Chinese that people thought that the Emperor of China himself had given Carstensen the idea for it. Andersen was in Tivoli on 11th October, 1843, and was at once imbued with the spirit of the pavilion. That evening he wrote in his diary: "Started on the Chinese fairy tale". The result was "The Nightingale", a story as topical as ever about how we worship technology, but despise nature – represented by the little grey bird with the beautiful voice. And yet it is the little bird that saves the Emperor's life.

Copenhagen at that time was surrounded by ramparts – which were not demolished until towards the end of Andersen's life. Until then, the city hardly changed at all. At sunset the city gates were locked and the keys handed over to the custody of the king until sunrise. It was said that he slept with them under his pillow.

Within the confines of the town the streets stank of filth and rubbish. A sewerage system was not introduced until as late as 1899 and, to help pedestrians, boards were laid across the deep gutters. It was under such a board that "The Steadfast Tin Soldier" stood and thought of the little ballerina and instead met the angry water rat.

Not only that, Copenhagen was also a dark town: train oil lamps were the only form of illumination. During the 50's,

Tivoli, which opened in 1843, was from the very start full of oriental magic. *The Chinese Bazaar*, with its slender columns and tender pastels, was one of the most beautiful buildings in the garden. The Emperor of China himself was supposed to have provided the idea for it.

It was in *Tivoli* that Andersen found the inspiration for *The Nightingale*. The original Chinese Bazaar is no longer there. The tea house *The Chinese Pagoda*, on the other hand, does exist. Its reflection in the lake contributes to the fairy-tale atmosphere of the garden.

however, they were gradually replaced by the more efficient gas lamps. Not until the 80's did Copenhageners make the acquaintance of the first electric arc lamps, which caused a major sensation. In "The Old Street Lamp", which is about an old train oil lamp that is ready for the scrap heap, Andersen gives an impression of how faint the light was from such a lamp: the three candidates to take over the job were a herring head, which can shine in the dark, a piece of old touchwood and a glowworm!

At the same time, the old street lamp is symbolic of every old-age pensioner's problems. The immediate future looks extremely uncertain. "Have you heard the story of the old street lamp? ... There was once a respectable old street lamp who had performed his duties for many, many years, but had now been declared to be too old-fashioned. This was the last evening that he would hang from the lamp post and illuminate the street; and he felt like a ballerina who was dancing for the last time and knew that tomorrow she would be a has-been. The lamp was very frightened of the coming day, for he knew that he would be going to the town hall for the first time. There he would be inspected by the 'six and thirty' men of the town council to see whether or not he was fit for further service..."

We are now in Vester Voldgade, which was built when the rampart was removed. Here, on the corner of Farvergade and diagonally facing Copenhagen Town Hall, stands Vartov – which in Hans Christian Andersen's time was an old-people's home. In "From a Window in Vartov" he writes about the life of an old maid.

"Looking out on the green embankment which surrounds Copenhagen, and which once formed part of its defences, stands a large red building with many windows. Potted alecost and southernwood grow in the windows. Poverty has stamped its mark on the building and it is poor old people who live here. This is Vartov. Look! There is an old maid leaning on the window sill. She pulls a dead leaf

Hans Christian Andersen's stories are full of details which bring them to life and create an atmosphere of intimacy. "Have you heard the story of ... ," he says, addressing the reader directly. *The Old Street Lamp* also starts this way. The lamp is personified so that we can all understand its problems. It is a shame that it is going to be thrown on the scrap heap, but it is also a shame that Copenhagen has to languish in the dark. "It was its last evening in the street; and tomorrow it would have to go to the town hall. Those were two dark thoughts for the lamp to think about, and so you can guess how it burned."

off the alecost and looks out at the green embankment where the children are playing merrily. What is she thinking about? The drama of a life unfolds within her thoughts.

"The poor children, how happily they play! What red cheeks, what bright eyes - and yet they have neither shoes nor socks to their feet. They dance on the green embankment ..."

From Vartov we continue down Vester Voldgade to Vestergade.

The present *Vartov* on the corner of *Farvergade* was built 1726-44 as a home for the old and infirm. The church was added in 1755; the writer N.F.S.Grundtvig was the vicar there 1839-72. In Andersen's time Vartov lay just across from the ramparts. In *From a Window in Vartov* it is described as "A large red building with many windows". Visitors are allowed to go in and admire the beautiful old courtyard.

Cribbley-Crabbley

To enter the city in those days one had to pass through Vesterport – The West Gate. Behind Vesterport lay Vestergade, which was the street for newly-arrived visitors. Hostels and taverns stood closely packed side by side. "Some of the travellers put up at 'Gardergaarden' ('The Guards' Inn') in Vestergade. I went there too. Having handed in my permit, I got a little room and was now, so it seemed to me, at the goal of my dreams."

Vestergade. It was here to No.18 -"The Guards' Inn" – that the gangling youth came, clutching his bundle of clothes, in search of lodgings. Look in through the gateway – there is still something left of the old atmosphere.

The Guards' Inn still existed in 1919, when this picture was taken. Then as now the building was in a sorry state. It was here that the young Andersen spent his first night in Copenhagen.

The area of Copenhagen within the ramparts, Christianshavn included, measured at that time 757 acres. Crowded together within that area were 120,000 people. Today the same area houses a population of no more than about 25,000.

Walking through the streets of Copenhagen in those days must have been like walking through the streets of some town in India: people everywhere, handcarts, horses and carriages, cows, pigs, hens. Noise. A town that must be every bit as full of opportunity as it was of people. All you had to do was to put your hand in the lucky dip. So must Hans Christian Andersen have thought on that memorable day in 1819. Later he came to regard Copenhagen as a spiritual prison, "Where houses stand like soldiers, where stairs and bay windows are trimmed" into cultivated streets, and where wild flowers such as himself felt ill at ease.

In "The Drop of Water" we see Copenhagen through the magnifying glass.

"It really looked like a whole town where everybody was running around with nothing on. It was horrible; but still more horrible was the sight of people pushing and elbowing one another, wrestling and wrangling, snapping and snarling. Those at the bottom had to be on top and those on top had to be at the bottom! 'Look! His leg is longer than mine! Pooh! Off with it! And there is someone with a little pimple behind his ear. An innocent little pimple. But it hurts him. And it's going to hurt him even more!' And they slashed at it and they pulled him about and they ate him just because of the little pimple. Another creature was sitting there as quiet as a young maid, wanting only to be left in peace. But the young maid had to come forward. And so they pulled her and they dragged her and they ate her right up!

'That is extremely funny!' said the magician.

'Yes, but what do you make of it?' asked Cribbley-Crabbley. 'Have you any idea what it is?'

'It's plain enough!' said the other. 'It's Copenhagen or some other big city. They all look alike. A big city anyway!'

'It's ditch-water!' said Cribbley-Crabbley."

Throw Him in Jail

In the story of "The Old Street Lamp", we have already heard of the 36 men of the town council. They corresponded to Copenhagen's Civic Council – even though there were actually no more than 32 men in this council! They met at Domhuset – The Courthouse – in Nytorv, where we are now standing. Their power dated back to the beginning of absolute monarchy in 1660. In acknowledgement of their active resistance during the Swedish siege of 1658-59, the middle classes had been granted special privileges by the king, and it was not until 1840 that the 32 were replaced by a democratically-elected city council.

It was perhaps this venerable council who – in "The Tinder-Box" – had

The Courthouse, built 1803-16, with its six mighty Ionic columns makes an impressive edifice. Perhaps it was here, in Andersen's imagination, that the soldier in *The Tinder-Box* was sentenced? The courthouse and the prison are linked by covered passages. The bridge across *Slutterigade* is known as *The Bridge of Sighs* due to the countless prisoners who have trudged their weary way to court. These days the house is used by the city court.

The prison in *Slutterigade* is reserved for trouble-makers, thieves, and robbers. Even today it is possible to imagine the soldier behind the thick bars in the basement cell, and the shoemaker's boy running past and losing one of his slippers through the bars – and then the soldier persuading the boy to fetch his tinder-box.

made themselves comfortable ready to see the soldier hanged. "Outside the town a high gallows had been built and round about it stood the soldiers and hundreds and hundreds of thousands of people. The king and queen sat on a beautiful throne opposite the judge and the whole assembled council."

When we look up at the Courthouse, we can sense the aura of power and authority emanating from the columns, underscored by the justice in the inscription, "Let law be the cornerstone of the land!" But suddenly the guardians of the treasure, the three large dogs, come bounding onto the scene, summoned by the soldier's tinder-box. And they can administer their own form of justice:

"Save me now from being hanged!" said the soldier; and the dogs flew at the judge and all the council, seized one by the legs, another by the nose and threw them so many fathoms into the air that they hit the ground and broke into little pieces."

But worse is yet to come. For the king and queen are also due to be sent flying, even though the king declares: "We refuse to...!" The soldier becomes a popular hero and wins the princess. The story of the spirited soldier is, in fact, nothing less than a revolution.

It must have been in the cells down in the basement just around the corner in Slutterigade that the soldier was thrown into jail. The windows there are at pavement level and, luckily, the shoemaker's boy lost one of his slippers so that it flew in through the iron bars.

The Inner City

From Nytorv we continue up Nørregade to Vor Frue Kirke (The Church of Our Lady), actually the Cathedral of Copenhagen, which stands opposite the University. The interior of the cathedral is extremely simple: the decoration consists mainly of the figures of Christ and the twelve Apostles, the work of Andersen's close friend, Bertel Thorvaldsen.

It was from here that Hans Christian Andersen's funeral procession started on 11th August, 1875 – one of the greatest funerals that the capital had ever witnessed. He was so well-known and loved that everybody felt that they had lost a close friend.

After the funeral ceremony, which was attended by the king and the crown prince, tens of thousands of Copenhageners followed the bier to the Assistens Cemetery in Nørrebro.

In this old cemetery many of Andersen's contemporaries have also been laid to rest – including those at whose dinner table he was a frequent guest. Today Assistens is more of a park than a cemetery and on a fine summer's day it is a favourite spot for sun worshippers.

From Frue Plads (the University Square), we continue along Store Kannikestræde to Købmagergade, which is one of the oldest and longest streets in the inner part of the city. It was also one of Andersen's favourite streets during his first years in Copenhagen. At that time the University Library was housed in the attic of Trinitatis Church behind the Round Tower. The librarian, Rasmus Nyerup, was the "provost" at Regensen, the students' residence opposite the Round Tower. Like the poet, he came from Odense, a fact which created a certain mutual sympathy.

"My curious nature appealed to the old man," Andersen relates, "and he took a liking to me. He let me go and look at the books in the library above the Round Church on condition that I 'put them back in the right place'. In this I was most conscientious and likewise took the greatest care of the illustrated books he let me borrow and take home with me."

Andersen's grave in the *Assistens Cemetery*. It was Edvard Collin who chose the burial place for Andersen, himself and his Henriette. Many years later there was criticism of the way the family had "taken over" the Poet, and the Collins' memorial stone was removed.

The portly lines of the Round Tower projected out into the street, no ordinary church tower by any standard. Christian IV's characteristic monogram and the date, 1642, gleam from the upper part of the tower. When the Russian Czar, Peter the Great, visited Copenhagen in 1716, he rode on horseback up the spiral passage inside the tower, followed by Czarina Catharina in a horse-drawn carriage.

From the top of the tower there is a view of far horizons and of near. From this vantage point, you might catch sight

The Round Tower seen from the courtyard of *Regensen*. The tower, 36 metres high, was built together with *Trinitatis Church* and was originally an observatory. The inscription at the top of the tower means: "Bring, O Lord, wisdom and justice to the heart of our crowned Christian IV."

The spiral passage-way inside the *Round Tower* goes from street-level right up to the gallery at the top. The Russian Czar, Peter the Great, thought it so intriguing that he rode all the way up on horseback. From the top there is a magnificent view of Hans Christian Andersen's Copenhagen.

The houses at *Gråbrødretorv* provide the best possible backdrop for an outdoor performance of Andersen's fairy tale, *Hans Clodhopper*. The square, with its many restaurants, has become a popular meeting place. In the Poet's day it was full of market stalls. The oldest houses are from the 1730's, after the great fire of 1728. Others were built after the British bombardment of 1807.

Copenhagen, e.g. here at *Gråbrødretorv*, is full of fairytale signboards. Just look up. Andersen is not without humour when, in *The Storm Changes the Signboards*, he makes the signboards of the town fly through the air and land again in the wrong places: "The cooper's barrel finds itself hanging outside a corset maker's", and the theatre where people never come gets a strange playbill: 'Horseradish Soup and Stuffed Cabbage' – but the people came!" notes the Poet.

of the Shepherdess and the Chimney Sweep. The two small porcelain sweethearts sit quite lost on one of the many chimneys, gazing out on the great, wide world.

Let us stay in the inner part of the city for a while to savour its atmosphere and all the experiences it has in store. During the light summer months, Gråbrødretorv, which we can get to via Skindergade, resounds to a raucous joie de vivre which is enjoyed by everyone but the residents. Here you will find restaurants to suit every pocket.

Walking back towards Købmagergade, you may wish to visit Valkendorfsgade Number 9, which is the home of the Danish Post and Telegraph Museum. Of particular interest are the models and pictures of the types of stagecoach which brought Andersen from Odense to Copenhagen in 1819 and which later took him on his innumerable travels to the many country houses in Denmark and to foreign parts.

The Danish Post and Telegraph Museum is open 13.00-16.00 on Tuesdays. Thursdays, Saturdays and Sundays.

The mail coach arrives at Vesterport 1845. On the left are the high ramparts which surrounded the city at that time. The picture is on display together with many others from the period at the *Danish Post and Telegraph Museum*.

Hans Christian Andersen's Flowers – and Bering's

In Andersen's day, No. 7 Købmagergade was a little shop selling puppets and puppet theatres. It was here at Blankensteiner and Son's that the 14-year-old boy would come to spend all his savings on a puppet's head or a picture. Then he would return to Dybensgade, where he lived at that time in a tiny rented room. There was so little space, in fact, that he had to sit up in bed to play with his puppet theatre – just as he had done in Odense. "I also made a peep-show and in this way played away a year of my youth."

For a long time after that, Blankensteiner's successor kept a glove shop – until the floral designer, Erik Bering, made Number 5 and Number 7 into one. Andersen's footprints must be cast in the concrete, for his spirit still lives there amid Bering's flowers.

Andersen's sense of decoration found expression in original bouquets, often consisting of modest specimens gathered on a stroll. The bouquets were a source of inspiration to him. Here Erik Bering has re-created a bouquet of heather wrapped in a paper cutting – an art which the Poet developed with the same imagination that he applied to his fairy tales.

Finn Rosted photo

Among the poet's many talents was also an instinct for using the abundance and diversity of Nature in original flower arrangements. Grasses, wild flowers, seed pods, cones, and herbs from the kitchen garden were arranged in bouquets together with prize blooms from the ornamental garden. Andersen's bouquets were renowned among his friends. "If we were alone in the garden, he would compose the most unusual bouquets I have ever seen," relates Axelline Lund, wife of the painter F.C.Lund.

The same might be said of Erik Bering's floral decorations, which are often inspired by the Poet. In 1978, when the 173rd anniversary of Andersen's birth was celebrated with a flower exhibition at the Museum of Fine Arts arranged according to the Poet's own notes, Erik Bering recreated Andersen's characteristic use of autumn flowers in vases from the 1800's. Bering's shop, however, is also a revelation of beauty on any ordinary day of the week, whether you wish to buy a bouquet or merely enjoy his window display. He shares with the Poet a love of nature which lasts throughout the twelve months of the year.

Here at *No.*7, *Købmagergade* Hans Christian Andersen pressed his nose against the window to look at Blankensteiner's puppets. Today people do the same to admire and choose from florist *Erik Bering's* cornucopia. The fairy-tale atmosphere of the old interior is present in full measure.

A Poet in the Walking Street

Strolling along Østergade has always been one of the pleasures of Copenhageners – and Hans Christian Andersen was often to be seen on "Strøget". When he was 24 years old, he wrote a poem in tribute to the street, "Østergade, Poetically Observed". The toy shop catches the "Child's Dreamy Gaze". The school (Efterslægtsselskabet's School – which stood on the site of what is now Illum's Department Store) teaches the children rational thought. The next phase is youth, which falls in love in Østergade and "Everything is so beautiful!"

But a look in at Watchmaker Jürgensen's tells us that time is passing. Before we know it, we are on our way to the pharmacy to buy the necessary medicaments of old age. Soon we are gone. "Alas! A tale so short to tell, but one short step – and then – our Østergade fare thee well!"

When, at the age of 14-15, Hans Christian Andersen walked along Strøget, the street did not yet bear the stamp of elegance which it was to acquire just ten years later. The shops were owned by small shopkeepers selling knitwear, wool and hosiery. Not until the 1830's did more fashionable shops start to appear. Peder Madsen's Passage, that lane so notorious for crime and prostitution, debouched into Østergade.

There was great poverty and distress in the Copenhagen of 1820, seven years after the national bankruptcy. For that reason, perhaps, the young poet did not stand out unduly from his surroundings as he walked along in other people's discarded clothes. His trousers were as narrow as drinking straws and too short. His waistcoat had once covered a much fatter paunch, and the top hat had long ago seen better days. A coat with a fox-fur collar did not fit him anywhere at all, but he was so proud of the collar that he was forever turning it out and adjusting it.

"Remember to be grateful," he wrote to himself in his diary.

Many a time, in the self-same diary, he would heave a sigh at his odd appearance, he who loved fine clothes.

"Every day I sat sewing puppet's clothes, and to get the coloured pieces of cloth I needed I used to go into the shops in Østergade and Kjøbmagergade and ask if they would give me some samples of cloth and ribbons. My imagination was so completely absorbed in this puppet finery that I often stopped in the street to gaze at the rich ladies in their silks and velvet, and in my mind I pictured all the royal cloaks, trains, and knightly garments I could make out of their clothes."

At this stage of his life, he was completely dependent on the charity of others. All the cast-off clothes he was given, all the economic help he received, all the gratitude he was supposed to show – it was almost too much. There are many ironic remarks about poverty and gratitude dotted around the fairy tales.

But at the beginning of the 1830's he started to earn money from his writing. And when, in 1838, the king awarded him a poet's salary of 400 rixdollars a year, his financial problems were really about to become a thing of the past. In a letter to a friend, Henriette Hanck, in Odense, he writes:

"What interests me at the moment is a Mackintosch *(sic)* I have acquired, and an elegant winter coat. This is the first winter that I appear in public as a human being. I have been padded and polished so that I look really fine. I am a dandy! And so one has to take a stroll up and down Østergade. And 'The Poet isn't ugly after all!' say the ladies, and fine ladies at that. They nudge each other in the ribs and stare. 'Look, it's the Poet!' they whisper. And so of course

The Royal Copenhagen sales rooms at *Amagertorv* are housed in a beautiful Renaissance building erected in 1616 during the reign of Christian IV. There are displays of faiance and porcelain throughout the building and on the second floor there is a cosy tea shop. The crowds of people in the square correspond to the street scenes of Andersen's day.

one puts on airs! This is the first summer and autumn that I have felt satisfied here at home and enjoy myself as I do when I am away. I have come to an understanding of myself and the world, and everything takes on a more secure appearance, a more serene light."

No sooner had the Poet returned from a journey abroad than he was out strolling along Østergade. "Rome has its Corso, Naples its Toledo ... Copenhagen has its Østergade. And in this street we will stay," he writes in "The Magic Galoshes". And Østergade has retained its atmosphere as a shopping street – even though the atmosphere of elegance has gone by the board. In 1962, Strøget was made into a walking street, with the pavement trading which that implies. Children and young people busk – perhaps to earn money to travel to foreign parts. Or perhaps towards an education? Perhaps someone or other will happen to come by who can see the fate of these youngsters and find room for them in a fairy tale – just as Andersen did in "The Little Match Girl".

Where Østergade merges into Amagertorv you will find the Royal Copenhagen sales rooms. Already in Andersen's time, the production of small porcelain figurines – artisans and dancers – had become a tradition. The Shepherdess and the Chimney Sweep stood on the sideboard in many a Copenhagen home. They became the main characters in one of the most beautiful and dramatic love stories the Poet wrote – "The Shepherdess and the Chimney Sweep".

The small figurines are still popular purchases. Go inside the shop, use your imagination – and see if you too become a poet in the Walking Street!

In the *Royal Copenhagen* windows, life on *Strøget* merges in with the Poet's figures and creates a harmony between past and present. The Poet himself sits discreetly in the background as if dreaming up a new fairy tale.

The Stairs of Fame

From Amagertorv we walk down to Højbro Plads and turn right into Gammel Strand, the old fish market recalled by the figure of the fisherwoman from Skovshoved. On the other side of the canal we can see Thorvaldsen's Museum. Before continuing along Nybrogade, you may wish to make a short detour. Turn right into the medieval town with its narrow streets to Badstuestræde, which is situated between Strøget and Kompagnistræde. In No.18, Badstuestræde lived the solo dancer Dahlén and his family. This was the first home to open its doors to the budding poet and Dahlén's wife took good motherly care of him – ably assisted by the daughters of the house. He felt at home with them. "I brought along my little theatre and peep-show; ran with it under my hostess's apron and played for Madam Dahlén, who was greatly amused by my naivety."

Dahlén was ballet master of the Royal Theatre ("Det Kongelige Teater"), whose ballet school was at that time housed at the Court Theatre ("Hofteatret"). To find this theatre, return to Nybrogade, turn left and cross over

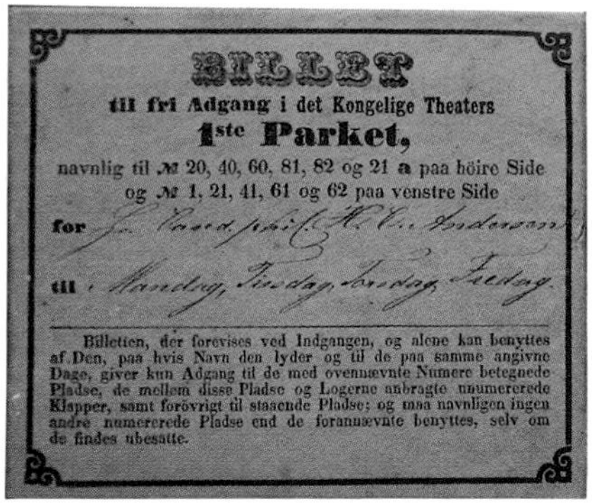

Andersen's two permanent complimentary tickets to the Royal Theatre and the Casino Theatre at the *Theatre Museum*. He retained his interest for the theatre throughout his life.

Stormbroen, walk down along Frederiksholm Kanal and turn left across the first bridge – "Marmorbroen". You then follow the arcade around to the right. No.18 is the Theatre Museum – in former times the Court Theatre.

It was Antoine Bournonville, father of the famous choreographer and ballet dancer, August Bournonville, who was head of the school. It was this man, then, that Andersen went to see in 1820 to seek admission. As Bournonville was in Paris, however, it was Dahlén who received him. He had already heard of this strange boy, and accepted him as a pupil.

"There I stood all morning at the long bar and stretched my legs and learned to do a *'battement'*, but despite my zeal and good will I did not show great promise as a dancer. Mr Dahlén declared that I was hardly likely to become anything more than a *'figurant'*."

In the story of "Lucky Peer", he returns to this experience. "He had to stand and stretch out his legs, holding on to a bar so as not to fall, while he learned to kick, first the right, then the left leg. It was not as difficult for him as it was for most of the others. The ballet master clapped at his performance and said that he would soon be in the ballet."

The pupils came in via No.14 or No.10, and there was a long passage to walk down before they reached the stairs leading to the stage. We have to imagine, then, the theatre full of children from the poorest districts of Copenhagen with wild dreams of a great and glorious future. It was here that August Bournonville performed his first dance solo at the age of nine. The later so celebrated actress, Johanne Luise Heiberg, stood as little Miss Pätges at the bar together with the young Andersen and Louise Rasmussen, who later married the King, Frederik VII. No wonder that these modest stairs came to be known as the Stairs of Fame.

The Stairs of Fame leading to the stage of the *Court Theatre* have been worn down over the years by the many hopeful would-be dancers. August Bournonville, the actress Johanne Luise Heiberg, Countess Danner, and Hans Christian Andersen were but a few of those who danced here as children. The stairs might still echo to their eager young voices.

There are not many Hans Christian Andersen exhibits in the museum, but in a glass case are his permanent complimentary tickets to Casino and the Royal Theatre. On the opposite wall hang portraits of Jenny Lind, the Swedish singer whom he courted. A contemporary poster on the wall tells us that in 1845 she appeared at the Court Theatre to raise money in aid of neglected children. In 1839, Andersen, already wrapped in the mantle of fame, read fairy tales here to students.

To be sure, his dreams of becoming a dancer, singer, or actor were never realised. But he celebrated triumphs as reader of his own works.

On special occasions, the Theatre Museum still provides the setting for theatrical arrangements. Singers, dancers, and lecturers all appear here and thus continue a century-old tradition, of which Hans Christian Andersen is also a part.

The Theatre Museum is open 14.00-16.00 on Wednesdays and 12.00-16.00 on Sundays.

Two Geniuses

Returning the way we came, we cross over Marmorbroen, turn right along Frederiksholms Kanal and then again right along the canal. There in front of us is Thorvaldsen's Museum. The building was designed by the architect G.Bindesbøll for Copenhagen Council to house the works

Thorvaldsen was given a royal welcome when he returned to Denmark to stay after many years in Rome. The occasion is depicted in *Jørgen Sonne's frieze* which covers three sides of the building. Here is part of the poets' boat with Andersen standing at the mast.

of art which the famous sculptor had donated to the city in 1838. The outside of the building is covered with a frieze depicting Thorvaldsen's homecoming. The frieze was painted from sketches by Jørgen Sonne and was reconstructed by Axel Salto in 1959 after more than a hundred years of erosion by wind and weather.

Bertel Thorvaldsen and Hans Christian Andersen's friendship arose way back in their young days when the sculptor had met Andersen in the street in Holmens Kanal and Thorvaldsen had enquired: "Where have I seen you before? I believe we know each other, don't we?" Later they had met in Rome and when, at the height of his fame after 40 years in Italy, Thorvaldsen had returned to Copenhagen, Andersen had been among the reception committee which sailed out to meet the frigate "Rota".

"Thorvaldsen was expected in Denmark in the autumn of 1838 ... It was a national festival. Boats bedecked with flowers and pennants bobbed on the water between Langelinie and Trekroner ... Some indication of all this can still be seen in the painted frieze on Thorvaldsen's Museum. In the poets' boat one recognises Oehlenschlæger, Heiberg, Hertz, and Grundtvig. I am standing on the thwart, holding on to the mast and waving my hat." Thorvaldsen died in 1844 and lies buried in the courtyard of the museum. And that is what the story of the sparrows, "The Neighbours", is about.

"There was a large house painted in many colours. It stood just next to the palace and the canal, where there were ships laden with apples and earthernware pots. The windows were wider at the bottom than at the top, and when the sparrows looked in, each room was like looking down into a tulip with every colour and embellishment imaginable. And in the middle of the tulip stood white people, they were of

Thorvaldsen's Museum, built 1848, surmounted by the Goddess of Victory driving her chariot. It is unusual for an individual artist to be given a whole museum all to himself, but Bertel Thorvaldsen - a European celebrity in his day - achieved that mark of distinction. Thorvaldsen made a great impression on Andersen and is mentioned in *The Fairy Tale of My Life*, *Children's Chatter* and *The Neighbours*.

marble, some of them were also of plaster that is, but it all comes to the same thing for a sparrow. On top of the house stood a metal chariot with metal horses and the Goddess of Victory, also of metal, driving them.

'How it shines! How it shines!' cried Miss Sparrow ... And she flew down into the courtyard, which was also magnificent; there were painted palms and branches up the walls and in the middle of the courtyard stood a flowering rose bush. The fresh branches and the many flowers on the bush hung down over a grave ... which concealed the great master who had shaped the marble pillars."

The story, "Children's Chatter", is also about Thorvaldsen, for "Out of real life grow precisely the most wondrous fairy tales."

"In the town there stood a magnificent house which was full of treasures that everyone wanted to see; even people from outside the town came in to see the house. Now, which of the children we have described do you think could call the house his or hers? Yes, it's an easy question, no perhaps not so easy after all. The house belonged to the poor little boy. He had become something after all, even though his name ended in 'sen' - Thorvaldsen."

Wasn't Andersen at the same time perhaps also thinking of himself? The fairy tale of his life was the most wondrous of all, even though his name ended in 'sen'. The children who had spoken contemptuously of 'sen' names were not really evil - the Poet had experienced too much to believe that. He ends the fairy tale in his own mild fashion: "And the other three children? ... They became kind and decent human beings, for they were basically good. What they had once thought and said was just - Children's Chatter."

Thorvaldsen's Museum is a house full of treasures - it houses the sculptor's works created throughout a long and rich artistic lifetime. The museum has, over the past many years, arranged a large number of interesting exhibitions, not only of Thorvaldsen's own works but also of his contemporary Danish and foreign colleagues. The museum is open daily 10.00-17.00 except Mondays.

Little Elves at Højbro

Our next objective is the corner house at No.21, Højbro Plads. To get there, cross over the canal at Højbro. From 1855 the house was owned by the trading firm of Moses and Son G.Melchior, who conducted their business transac-

The balcony belonging to the Melchiors' apartment at *No. 21, Højbro Plads*. Here the Poet would often stand and admire the view of the canals and the palace. *The Wild Swans* flying past are part of a carnival procession with Andersen's fairy tales as its theme. Even today Copenhagen's inhabitants still help to make it a fairy-tale city. If the gateway to No.21 is open, take a look inside at the courtyard; it hasn't changed much.

tions from this address. On the second floor were the apartments of Moritz Melchior, the senior partner, and his wife Dorothea. Their home was the focal point for many of the personalities of the time in the world of art, music, and literature. Among them Andersen was a particularly dear friend who was virtually a daily visitor. The fact that he felt at home here he expressed gracefully on Mrs Melchior's fan:

"At Højbro Plads on the second floor,
the little elves dance for Mrs Melchior!"

The houses are built close together in this part of the town, the courtyards are narrow and, now as then, the characteristic outline of Nikolaj Church's tower rises above its surroundings. From the balcony on the second floor there is a view of the bustling square and the bridge leading across the canal to Christiansborg Slotsplads, the Stock Exchange, and further out to Knippelsbro. Andersen loved an unimpeded view in every sense of the word. For that reason pettiness affected him twice as deeply when he experienced it. And it is true that he became famous much more quickly abroad.

"I came to Copenhagen. A few hours later, I was standing at my window looking out when two well-dressed gentlemen came by. They saw me, stopped and laughed, and one of them pointed up and said loud enough for me to hear every word: 'Will you look, there's our orangutang who is so famous abroad' – It was crude, it was evil, it pierced my heart – it cannot be forgotten!"

The Melchior family celebrated the Poet's 70th birthday with a party that exceeded his wildest dreams. At the table the ageing Poet sat happy and deeply moved while loving tributes in the form of music and speeches were heaped upon him. The entire menu was composed with references to his fairy tales. It read as follows:

DINER
2den April 1875

"The Neighbours" (*Oysters*)
"Soup On A Sausage Pin"
"From The Duckyard" (*Turkeys*)
"Under The Willow Tree" (*Mushrooms*)
"A Question Of Imagination" (*Baked Sweetbreads*)
"Five Peas From One Pod" (*With Green Peas*)
"Something" (*Salmon and Asparagus*)
"The Sweethearts" (*Wine Jelly*)
"The Wild Swans" (*Wildfowl*)
"Everything In Its Right Place"
(*Buttered Bread And Cheese*)
"Ask The Costermonger" (*Celery And Radishes*)
"The Ice Maiden" and "The Snowman"
"Lovely!" (*Dessert*)

Something from
"The Neck Of The Bottle"

"The Old House" (*Château Guirand*)
"From Spain" (*Sherry*)
"The High Jumpers" (*Champagne*)
"It Is Perfectly True" (*Bordeaux*)
"The Most Beautiful Rose In The World"
(*Château Larose*)
"She Was No Good" (*Madeira*)
"Auntie" (*Veuve Clicquot*)
"Hidden But Not Forgotten" (*Old Madeira*)
"The Last Pearl" (*Malvasier*)

The Melchiors' sitting room opening out onto the balcony looks more or less the same as it did in the Poet's time. The white-tiled stove was in those days hidden behind the famous screen depicting in collage form the story of his life. Today the screen is at the Hans Christian Andersen Museum in Odense. In this apartment at *Højbro Plads* the Poet as an old man used to come to dinner on Thursdays, and it was here that his 70th birthday was celebrated.

It was also Moritz and Dorothea Melchior who took the initiative to have a statue made of Andersen while he was still alive in order that he might have a say in deciding how it should look. The idea, although not new, was realised in 1874, the project being financed by a large-scale collection throughout the country from the Royal Household to schoolchildren.

Among the sculptors who came under consideration, August Saabye emerged the winner. Andersen could not abide him. Ill as he was in the last year of his life, he was constantly obliged to "pose for his statue", and when Saabye placed a child between the knees of the model, Andersen became really angry:

"I then said clearly and unequivocally that I was very dissatisfied with his statue of me, that neither he nor any of the other sculptors knew me or had seen me read, that I could not bear anyone behind me, that I did not have children either on my back or on my lap; that my fairy tales were just as much for grown-ups as for children; the latter saw nothing but the ornamentation and only when they became mature adults could they perceive the whole story. That the naive element was only a part of my fairy tales, that humour was actually the salt in them."

Andersen had his way. There are no children in his vicinity, he sits with book in hand and tells his story, and often receives the company of seagulls, which perch on the top of his head or his outstretched hand.

Andersen did not live to see the finished statue. He died in 1875 and it was not until June, 1880, that the monument in Kongens Have was unveiled. Since then, the spot has become a favourite place for children to play, and to that the old Poet can surely have no objection.

The statue of Andersen by August Saabye was completed while the Poet was still alive, but was not erected in *Kongens Have* until 1880. There he sits in the surroundings that provided the first inspiration for his fairy tales.

Riborg Voigt and Jenny Lind

On the corner of Fortunstræde and Ved Stranden stands Domus Technica. This building has a long history. The "Fortunen" establishment goes back to around 1850, but from 1750 until then it was the home of the "Hotel Royal" and the restaurant, "Den Gyldne Fortun". The hotel held many tender memories for Andersen. In 1830, his first love, the Funen girl Riborg Voigt, stayed here with her family – he met her here through her brother Christian, a good friend of his. It was also here that he experienced a new love in the Swedish nightingale, Jenny Lind. He met her in September, 1843, at the house of the ballet master August Bournonville, who lived on the corner of Fortunstræde and Nikolai Plads – the house has long since been pulled down – and immediately lost his heart to her. The

These beautiful lamps belong to *No. 18, Ved Stranden* the address of *Den Gyldne Fortun* – formerly Hotel Royal. At the corner table in the restaurant Andersen ate his famous farewell dinners with Riborg Voigt and Jenny Lind. A corner of the Melchior family's house, No.21, Højbro Plads can be seen in the background.

Riborg Voigt (1806-83)

Jenny Lind (1820-87)

week after he was already thinking of proposing, but she did not reciprocate his feelings.

When she was in Copenhagen again, in 1845, she gave a dinner for her friends at the Hotel Royal, today "Den Gyldne Fortun", where she proposed a toast to him as a brother. This made a deep impression on him. "For a time no books, no people had a better, a more ennobling influence on me as a Poet than Jenny Lind."

"Den Gyldne Fortun" is still a restaurant to this day and if you ask, the staff will be pleased to point out the table where the Poet and the singer once sat side by side.

The Red Lantern District

From Højbro Plads we continue along Fortunstræde and turn right into Admiralgade which, in turn, leads us to Dybensgade. Notice the cobblestones and the old street lamps which, especially in the evening, evoke a special atmosphere. Walk down to the corner house, No.20 Dybensgade. It was here, in 1820, that Andersen rented a room from Madam Henckel, the widow of a ship's first mate. "The room she gave me was in fact no more than an empty larder without a window and with no more daylight than that which came in through the open door from the kitchen. But I might, she said, sit in her parlour as much as I liked." The original house still stands, apparently unchanged.

Continue along Dybensgade and cross Bremerholm, which was formerly Ulkegade, later Holmensgade. In this dirty, foulsmelling robbers' den of iniquity (in those days, that is!) Andersen lived from September, 1819, apparently without noticing what actually went on in the street. His next landlady in

Dybensgade was one of the most wretched districts in 19th-century Copenhagen.

Ulkegade, Madam Thorgesen, let him have, "A little room without windows, actually a larder near the kitchen with two air holes in the door. There was only room for the bed and two chairs, one placed on top of the other. In what was left of the room I could just manage to stand and get dressed or undressed."

The house in Ulkegade was demolished long ago. The site is now occupied by Magasin's multi-storey car park.

From Dybensgade turn left into Asylgade and up to Vingårdsstræde. Even though Andersen's lodgings were miserable, he nevertheless lived very centrally. In No.5, Vingårdsstræde lived singing master Guiseppe Siboni, whom Andersen visited full of hope on 18th September, just after his arrival in Copenhagen.

"He just happened to be giving a big dinner party. Our famous composer, Professor Weyse, the poet Baggesen, and numerous others were there." The young Andersen told the housekeeper the entire story of his life and she must have gone in and told the whole company for they all came trooping out. The end of the story was that Siboni, moved by the young man's desperate plight, promised to train his voice, and Weyse collected money for him, which he went to receive the following day.

For three quarters of a year he went to Siboni for singing lessons, and thus the fairy tale of his life started to take shape. In 1827, when he was back in Vingårdsstræde – this time to take his school-leaving examination – he was given lodgings in the attic of No.6 by the widow, Kirstine Schwarz, who herself rented rooms from distiller P.M. Spendrup. Here he felt at home. "High up under the eaves, where the swallow lives, the student too has his lodging," he wrote in a poem. This little attic room lives on both in the novel, "Only A Fiddler" and in "A Picture Book Without Pictures", but it can also pop up in the fairy tales.

"There was once a real student, he lived in the attic and didn't own a thing." The student from "The Pixie And The Grocer" who sets more store by poetry than a piece of cheese is the Poet himself. And perhaps we can recognise him again as the soldier in "The Tinder-Box" who had to move to an attic room, "A tiny, little attic right up under the roof ... and none of his friends came to see him because there were such a lot of stairs to climb."

In "A Picture Book Without Pictures" the room plays an integral part:

"I am a poor lad, I live in one of the narrowest streets, but I am not short of light because I live high up with a view across all the roofs. The first few days after I had come here to the city, it all seemed cramped and lonely; instead of the forest and the green hills I now had only the grey chimneys for a horizon. Not a friend did I have here, not a familiar face greeted me.

One evening I was standing quite mournfully at my window. I opened it and looked out. Oh, how happy I became! I saw a face I knew – a round, friendly face, my best friend from back home: it was the moon, the dear old moon."

It was also here that he found the inspiration for his first Copenhagen prose work, "A Journey on Foot to Amager". It starts as follows, "On New Year's Eve I sat quite alone in my little room, looking out across the snow-clad roofs of all the neighbouring houses; then the evil spirit, which we call Satan, rushed through me and inspired me with the sinful thought of becoming a writer."

The Poet's student garret has been preserved in its original form. Today it stands untouched, and tourists from all over the world flock like pilgrims to imbibe the atmosphere of the place. It is open during normal business hours for viewing by appointment. Since 1917, incidentally, the whole Vingårdsstræde court, with its medieval cellars and the beautiful Magasin Hall with its Corinthian columns, has been owned by Magasin. Today the cellars have been transformed into an exclusive restaurant named after the first royal owner of the house, King Hans.

No. 6, Vingårdsstræde. In this small garret the young student lived and wrote his first romantic works. Today it is owned by *Magasin*. It is the only one of all Andersen's rented rooms which not only still exists, but in all its emptiness remains almost unchanged – an attraction which should not be missed.

A Chimney Fire – and Love

On 1st December, 1838, Andersen moved into the Hotel du Nord, which was situated on the corner of Vingårdsstræde and Kongens Nytorv and was later to become the department store Magasin du Nord. There he was a permanent resident until May 1847, living in two attic rooms – one facing the yard and one looking out onto the street just across from the Royal Theatre. It suited him being near the theatre, and life at the hotel let him imagine: now you are on your travels.

In a letter to his good friend, Henriette Hanck, he gives a detailed description of his new residence, "My living room is cosy. Here is a plan of it: No.1, Window to Kongens Nytorv with raised floor and chairs. No.2, A bureau

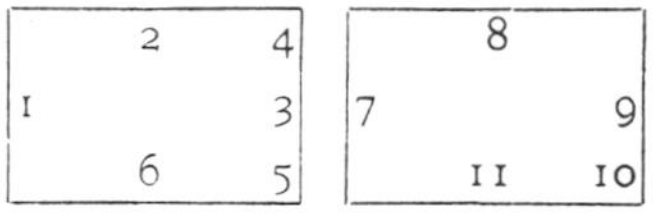

with Thorvaldsen's bust and paintings on the walls. No.3, Door to the passage. No.4, My bookshelves with my bust, a crucifix, and several curiosities. No.5, Stove. No.6, Sofa with a table in front of it, covered with a green cloth. Above the sofa is an oval mirror. Now we cross the passage to the bedroom, which faces the yard. No.7 is the door, 8 the bed, 9 the window with table and chairs in front, 10 stove, 11 bookcase, 12 food cupboard."

He is pleased with the good service. When he rings, the servants come, "One blacker than the one before, which must have a beneficial influence now that I am writing

Hotel du Nord in 1834. The Poet lived in the attic with a view of the Royal Theatre across the street.

The chimneys of the town were the inspiration for *The Shepherdess and the Chimney Sweep.* Here seen from the Round Tower.

'The Mulatto'." In a light-hearted mood he makes an ink blot and finishes, "Please excuse the last ink blot, though ... the colour is that of my Mulatto!"

His daily routine follows a fixed pattern, "8 o'clock: coffee, after which I read and write until 11 or 12 o'clock, then walk to the Association (The Students' Association) to read the newspapers, then a bath, a stroll, and visits until 3 o'clock. Now a rest, 4 to 6 o'clock dinner and the rest of the day at home to work or read: if there is something new on at the theatre, I will be there, nowhere else in the evening."

He also receives visitors. In a letter to Henriette Hanck he invites her, together with Mrs Signe Læssøe, to pay him a visit. Ingeborg and Louise Collin have already been there. "You will see I can produce a coffee table. I have a black waiter who will serve you your coffee. A piece of Holmens Kanal, The Theatre and the Square are my view. And what is even better: up above a smithy's chimney I can see the sea, the dear billowing sea."

These years at the Hotel du Nord are among the best in his life, from both a human and an artistic point of view. His financial circumstances are in order, and the ideas pour forth. In 1836, he writes his novel, "O.T.", in 1837 "Only a Fiddler", and every year a new collection of fairy tales.

The Poet is inspired by the slightest things, "Fire in the stove pipe. The Shepherdess And The Chimney Sweep", he writes in his diary.

Perhaps it is the chimney mentioned earlier which becomes the escape route for the loving porcelain couple out into the great big world. But every bit as happy as the Poet is with his view of the great, wide world, just as unhappy is the little shepherdess:

"There was the sky with all its stars overhead, and all the roofs of the city below. They could see so far around them, far out into the world; the poor shepherdess had never imagined it would be like that. She laid her little head up against her chimney sweep and wept so much that the gold ran from her sash.

'It's all too much!' she cried. 'I can't stand it! The world is much too big! If only I was back on the little table under the mirror again! I will never be happy until I am there again! Now that I have come with you into the big wide world, now you can take me home again, if you love me at all!'

But here again the naive Poet did not realise what was going on around him. And the rumours of hotel owner Rasmus Jørgensen's unsavoury dealings were surely flying thick and fast enough, so that no-one was surprised when, in 1859, he was brought to justice and convicted of, among other offences, the letting of rooms for immoral purposes. Brothel du Nord was the popular name of the establishment.

And so it ceased to be a hotel. In 1893 Magasin du Nord was completed in French mansion house style. A small "Hotel du Nord" high up on frontage is the only reminder of its past.

Around Kongens Nytorv

In 1866 Andersen returned home from his long journey to Holland, Belgium, France, Spain, and Portugal, and had to find a new place to live. Miss Thora Hallager in No.1, Lille Kongensgade had two spare rooms on the second floor which were just to his taste. "On my return to Copenhagen I moved into my present residence at Kongens Nytorv, Copenhagen's most beautiful square with the Royal Theatre, one of the least beautiful buildings, just outside. But if the shell is bad, the kernel is good and many memories are attached to it."

Here, on the corner of Restaurant à Porta, he lived for almost three years, until July 1869. From here he could cut straight across the street to the Royal Theatre, nor was it far to the Casino Theatre in Amaliegade:

"On the ground floor is one of the city's most frequented cafés, on the first floor a restaurant, on the second floor a club, on the third floor, where I have my apartment, there is also a doctor, and above me there is a photographer's studio. One can see then that I have food and drink close at hand, that I cannot want for company, cannot die without medical help, and that the photographer can keep my picture for posterity, that is what one can call being well situated. My small rooms, I have only two, are cosy, sunny, and decorated with pictures, books, statuettes and, as my lady friends in particular ensure, always flowers and greenery. At the Royal Theatre and Casino Theatre I have my good seat every evening, every social class is well disposed towards me, gracious enough to admit me to their circle."

à Porta's café and restaurant still exist at street level, if with somewhat different décor. The interior has beautiful gilt-leather tapestries. On the walls are prints from the restaurant's long history, which goes right back to 1788, when a Swiss man, Soltani, opened the first *conditori* in

à Porta Café & Restaurant 1898

Copenhagen. The present late-classical building was built in 1857 for pastry cook Stefan à Porta.

On the other side of Lille Kongensgade is another of Copenhagen's old attractions, Hviids Vinstue, the oldest wine bar in the town, dating back to 1723. Here too the walls are bedecked with prints and sketches of Copenhagen in the old days.

Whether or not Andersen ever set foot inside Hviids Vinstue he does not relate. It is known, however, that he stayed at Hotel d'Angleterre – and that on a number of occasions.

"I moved to Hotel d'Angleterre and was given number

Restaurant à Porta at *Kongens Nytorv* on the corner of *Lille Kongensgade*. While Andersen's rooms have long since vanished, the ground-floor restaurant still exists. The gilt-leather clad walls are decorated with prints from the old Copenhagen. The interior and the lighting produce an atmosphere reminiscent of Andersen's time. Andersen wrote of the place: "On the ground floor is one of the city's biggest and busiest cafés" – and that's the way it is today.

65 ... where it was as if a nightmare had come to an end. I felt rejuvenated, felt as if I was on my travels, felt as if I were back in a younger period. It was so beautiful, a wide view of the square, down Nyhavn and along Store Kongensgade."

Hans Christian Andersen actually lived all the way round Kongens Nytorv: at Hotel du Nord, in the à Porta building, at d'Angleterre, in Store Kongensgade, at three addresses in Nyhavn and in Tordenskjoldsgade.

Copenhagen was a constant inspiration. The Poet was a keen observer, but it is no ordinary Copenhagen vignette that emerges from his writings. Some authors' descriptions are so accurate that we are told not only what the houses and the streets looked like, but also what people ate and drank in the pubs. Not so Andersen. His Copenhagen is a puddle, an open window, a gutter for Kaj and little Gerda's roses, the shepherdess and the chimney sweep's chimney, a tin soldier under a gutter board. Everything he saw could set his imagination working. He himself said that the slightest incidents would evoke all sorts of images inside his head. Just walking across Kongens Nytorv he experienced so much that when he related what he had seen to his friends, they would slap their thighs and shout: "I don't believe it, the devil take me, I don't believe it, nothing like that ever happens to the rest of us." It might be anything at all, some episode, a cart that had overturned, spilling potatoes into the street. Anything and everything appealed to the Poet's sense of humour. And the story became better than ever when Andersen later retold it and added his friends' reactions. Then people would laugh so much that they almost fell out of their chairs.

Kongens Nytorv has always been fringed with stately buildings, some of which were noblemen's mansions in their time. Down along Nyhavn the sailing ships lay closely berthed and further out there was a view of the Sound.

Today the square still has an air of grandeur: an ultra-modern department store, a hotel first-class, an embassy, the Royal Academy of Fine Arts with its exhibition rooms, the Royal Theatre, large business concerns – yes, a stroll round the sides of the square is certainly worth the effort.

Kongens Nytorv is rightly called Copenhagen's most beautiful square – especially on a morning in May when the trees are just in leaf. In the background, *Hotel d'Angleterre* – where Andersen stayed on a number of occasions. The buildings around the square have changed little since the last years of Andersen's life.

The Royal Theatre

From his very first day in Copenhagen, the Royal Theatre exerted the greatest attraction on Andersen. It was there that he wished to become a success, and he had often imagined the bliss it would be when he finally stood before it. Already in the evening on 6th September, 1819, he went there.

"I walked around it several times, looked up at its walls and regarded it almost as a home. One of the ticket sellers who walks around here daily noticed me and asked if I would like a ticket. I was so completely innocent that I thought the man wanted to give me one and I thanked him profusely. He thought I was making fun of him and became angry, so I took fright and ran away from that place which was the dearest to me in this city."

A great theatrical career, no matter what – as a dancer, a singer, or an actor – that was his burning desire. As we already know, he was accepted by ballet master Dahlén and, on 25th January, 1821, he danced the role of a musician who was supposed to play for Nina in Galeotti's opera of the same name. "It was my début ... most likely I cut a comic figure." Just three months later, however, he was on the stage again. It was on 12th April in the ballet "Armida", where he appeared as one of the demonic mountain trolls. This time, moreover, his name appeared in the programme: "A Troll ... Hr.Andersen." "It was a great moment in my life that my name was now in print, and I thought it meant a halo of immortality for me. I took the ballet programme to bed with me at night, lay near the candle and stared at my name, put the programme down, only to pick it up again. It was blissful joy!"

Indeed, and it was also blissful joy eight years later when again he saw his name in the programme, now, however, as a writer. It was on the occasion of the performance of his little vaudeville, "Love in Saint Nicolas' Tower". Quite a

The Royal Theatre, built 1748, pulled down 1874. This was the goal of all the Poet's artistic dreams.

The Royal Theatre's auditorium 1857. The Acropolis Curtain – possibly the oldest in the world – is the same today as in the 19th-century Royal Theatre. For Andersen the Muses' temple was at Kongens Nytorv, for which reason he always chose to live nearby. When he wasn't away on his travels, he would go to the theatre every single day. Naturally he had his permanent seat in the stalls. Notice the Royal Box which, in those days too, was on the left.

few of his fellow students were in the theatre, and they applauded him enthusiastically. Overcome with joy, he rushed across to Mrs Collin's house to tell her that he was a success! And throughout the 1829-30 season he had a free ticket to the theatre.

He wrote in all 28 dramatic works for the stage. The Royal Theatre performed both "The Moorish Girl" and "The Mulatto", but it was at the Casino Theatre that he celebrated his greatest triumphs with his fairy-tale comedies.

As a theatrical writer he naturally had his own ironic relationship to the capricious public. In "The Storm Changes The Signboards", the wind changes the town's signboards around, and the theatre too acquires a new signboard on this occasion:

"The restaurant's menu, which hung in a heavy frame by the door, was placed by the wind just above the entrance to the theatre, to which people usually never went. It was a strange bill: 'Horseradish Soup and Stuffed Cabbage', but people came!"

The Poet's permanent seat every evening throughout the season was in the front stalls. In the story of "Auntie", however, it was not there that he placed this theatrical fanatic who, like the Poet himself, liked to go to the theatre every evening if possible. To get the most out of the performance, according to her, one had to sit, "Second tier, left side, the scenery looks best from there. It is always placed so that it looks best from the side with the royal box."

The Royal Theatre had been part of Kongens Nytorv since 1748. For a long time there had been agreement that the building was too small and, at the beginning of the 1870's, work was started on a new theatre just next door – the one that stands there today. In June, 1874, the last performance was given in the old theatre and, on 15th October the same year, the new building was inaugurated. Hans Christian Andersen was, of course, present:

"Outside large crowds had gathered already by 6 o'clock. All the houses round the square were illuminated; at the top of the theatre small gas lights burned. It was difficult to get across the street for people. Henriques and I went through the confectioner's rooms, which was a slightly shorter way than going out through the gate. We got there safe and sound. The corridors were heated and decorated with trees and flowers ... the theatre looked magnificent with the bright illumination and the ladies and gentlemen in all their finery. When the King came, the people in all the boxes rose to their feet. The prologue moved me, but particularly so when the audience rose and joined in with address to the royal box ... During the song I burst into tears. Niels Gade tried to cheer me up. 'Forget it now! Be merry again'. At supper I was in particularly fine fettle, a calm had come over me, I felt as if I had entered the new era, grateful to God and happy."

Until towards the middle of the 1800's , many of the theatre's seats were not numbered. This applied, for example, to the standing room in the pit – whose patrons would gather in front of the theatre early in the afternoon ready, when the doors opened, to charge into the theatre and do battle to get the places at the front of the pit.

The new *Royal Theatre* opened on 15th October, 1874. The theatre was brightly lit already at 6 o'clock when the audience, in their finest evening dress, crowded in. Andersen was there too of course. The curtain rose on ballet master August Bournonville's Holberg Apotheosis, after which there was a performance of a comedy by Ludvig Holberg – the Danish national playwright. Today the Royal Theatre is known as "The Old Stage" – as opposed to "The New Stage" (also known as "The Nest Box") which is to the left under the arch.

All three art forms – opera, ballet, and theatre – are performed on "The Old Stage".

Intermezzo in Tordenskjoldsgade

Along the left side of The Royal Theatre runs Tordenskjoldsgade, a street which did not exist when Hans Christian Andersen came to Copenhagen. It did not come into being, in fact, until after 1859 – when the Navy's Gammelholm yards closed down and Copenhagen Council built streets on the site – named, of course, after naval heroes.

The building was no more than three years old when, on 19th September, 1870, the Poet took up lodgings in Misses Charlotte and Emerentze Rossing's *hôtel garni* "Kronprinsesse Lovisa" – two rooms on the first floor above the gate at 30 rixdollars a month.

His fellow poet, Sophus Schandorph, who visited him there, gives a brief description of the "Neat, clean room with blue wallpaper and some bookshelves. There was something melancholy in the impression I received of his daily surroundings. Our most famous author, whose name is always mentioned outside Denmark as being representative of our writing, was living in this *hôtel garni* where everything looked so cold and boring."

Andersen, however, was quite happy, for he was in the middle of a creative period. He was writing his little novel, "Lucky Peer", from which he read aloud both at the Students' Association and to friends. It was published in November by Reitzel's Publishers. The plot in "Lucky Peer" sticks closely to Andersen's own youthful years. The poor boy Peer becomes first a child ballet dancer, then a singer, and climbs towards the stars in a meteoric career. In his moment of triumph he sings Aladdin in the opera of the same name and, as the happy-go-lucky son of fortune, experiences the culmination of success in the enthusiasm which embraces him – and immediately falls down dead on the stage.

"The happy soul chosen among millions," concludes the now 65-year-old Poet.

The story of "Auntie Toothache" is clearly inspired by this address.

"I am living with a quiet family. They don't worry about me even when I ring three times. Otherwise the house is a regular bedlam with all the hubbub of wind and weather and people. I live just above the gateway. Every cart that drives out or in sets the pictures swinging on the walls. The gate bangs and shakes the house as if there were an earthquake. If I am lying in bed, the shocks go right through my body, although they say it strengthens the nerves. When it's windy – and it's always windy in this country – then the long window – catches outside swing to and fro and bang against the wall. The gate bell to the yard next door rings at every gust of wind."

Soon Andersen moved again, this time to Hotel d'Angleterre "Where it was as if a nightmare had come to an end", he writes in his diary.

The house in Tordenskjoldsgade looks much as it did when the Poet lived there, except that today it has been painted white. There is a commemorative plaque with the inscription: "The Poet Hans Christian Andersen lived here from 1870 to 1871."

No.20 Nyhavn. The First Fairy Tales

We now return to Kongens Nytorv, walk past Charlottenborg, turn right into Nyhavn and walk down to No.20. After his first long journey abroad, Andersen took up residence here in 1834. A commemorative plaque tells us that it was here, in 1835, that he wrote his first collection of fairy tales. It contained "The Tinder-Box", "The Princess And The Pea", "Little Claus And Big Claus" and "Little Ida's Flowers". He loved living in Nyhavn. On one side he had a view of the canal and all the ships, on the other side the botanical garden behind Charlottenborg.

Two of Andersen's homes in *Nyhavn*. As a young man he lived in No.20, as an old man in No.18.

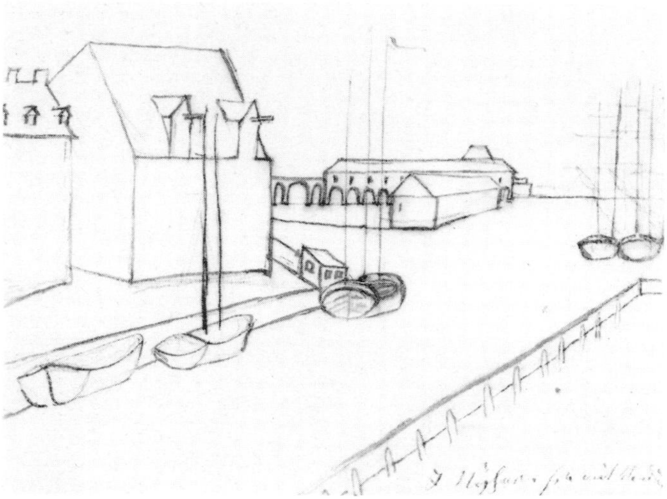

In Nyhavn from my Window. Drawing by Andersen from No.20, Nyhavn c.1834.

The view of *Nyhavn* from the ground-floor window is the same today as it was in the Poet's time.

"My bedroom ... faces south. The botanical garden unfurls like a green Lombardy plain behind the Alpine peaks of the courtyard wall. In the garden stands a tall, leafy poplar. In the moonlight it looks quite black and I come to think of the dark cypresses and all the beautiful things I dreamt of recently." ... "A large courtyard with two gates, situated in Nyhavn. You go up the stairs to the second floor, my name is on the door. You step inside – my apologies – into my bedroom – a long bed, bookshelves full of papers, a green cloth concealing my wardrobe, tables, chairs, and a stove are all the furniture there is ... The views from the windows are across the yard to the botanical garden with its trees and walks. The Stock Exchange spire and the tops of the ships' masts at Knippelsbro complete the background. Now we enter my study. There is a fire burning in the stove! On a little table are my cups and glasses together with an Italian crucifix which, in true Catholic fashion, I have decorated for this Christmas with silk ribbons. Then there are my bookshelves and other furniture, and out through the window we can see the three-masted ships and the boats scurrying past one another. If I lean my head out of the window, I can see beyond the warehouses to the Sound or, in the other direction, part of Kongens Nytorv..."

To begin with Andersen himself did not consider the fairy tales of any importance. Perhaps he thought they were too easy to write. "Little Ida's Flowers", for example, came into being during a visit to Charlottenborg. There his friend J.M.Thiele lived with his little daughter. A ray of sunshine, a glance out of the window at the profusion of flowers – that was all it took. That was how little Ida was given her own fairy tale and she and her dolls were immortalised – to the delight of children all over the world.

The botanical garden has shrunk considerably in size since then and is now kept locked. Only painters and sculptors from the Academy of Fine Arts have access to it. It is possible, however, to enter Charlottenborg's courtyard via

Even though there are no reminders left from Andersen's time, the stairs in *Boel's Gård* are the same as they were then. As soon as your hand slides along the banister and touches the door handles, you are transported back in time. Look inside at the old courtyards which have been painstakingly restored.

the gate in Nyhavn. The garden is at the far end behind the railings. In summer, when the garden is overgrown and the sculptors are out there working, the impression is a fine blend of art and nature.

The house at No.20, Nyhavn, was built in 1756 by the merchant Anders Bodenhoff. Today it is owned by Boel Foods Ltd, whose cheeses are sold all over the world.

The house has been beautifully restored. Between the front and the back house there is a cobbled courtyard. Hans Christian Andersen's rooms are now offices, but the windows through which the Poet observed life in Nyhavn have been retained.

He Never Ate at Home

It was an old tradition that families gave poor young people a seat at their dinner table so that they were sure of a decent meal at least once a day. Andersen too, in his young days, went the rounds of Copenhagen families. And since he never married and had a family himself, throughout the week he was a dear and cherished dinner guest within his circle of friends. "4 o'clock to 6 o'clock dinner," writes the 33-year-old poet in his diary.

"The Swineherd" takes place in quite a modest little kingdom. The young prince gets himself a job in the pigsty – because there were such a lot of pigs! He is something of an artist and fashions a lovely little cooking pot.

"As soon as the pot boiled, the bells tinkled so charmingly and played the old melody, 'Ach, du lieber Augustin'. But the most curious thing of all was that when you held your finger in the steam from the pot, you could at once smell what food was cooking on every hob in town."

If anyone knew what people had for dinner in Copenhagen, it was Hans Christian Andersen. He was still living in No.20, Nyhavn, when, in 1838, he wrote a description of his weekly dinner route.

"My dinners are: Monday at Mrs. Bügel's, where we always eat as if it were a large dinner party."

Mrs Bügel, who lived at No.12, Gammel Strand, was a rich 70 year-old wholesaler's widow who had taken a fancy to the Poet. It was a strange acquaintanceship. "On account of one of my poems, the old lady had taken a particular liking to me. I went there and from that day on she has virtually overwhelmed me with attention and courtesies. I am invited to her house every other minute, she sends me Italian wines, fruit – and recently a splendid Parisian dressing gown: a yellow background with red roses, a purple silk belt and collar." The Collin family teased him that he would end up marrying the widow.

"Tuesday with the Collins, where the eldest son and his wife also eat on this day, for which reason we always have something unusual."

Hans Christian Andersen's close connections to the Collin family started in 1822 when the influential Jonas Collin, a member of the board of directors of the Royal Theatre, took him under his wing. It was Collin who ensured that Andersen went to school and took his school-leaving examination. Now he was regarded as one of the family and virtually a brother to the other five children – two daughters and three sons. It was in that very year, 1838, that the Collins had moved house from No.2, Bredgade, to No.9, Amaliegade.

"Wednesday at the Ørsteds, who always receive their guests on that day."

The physicist H.C.Ørsted, the discoverer of electromagnetism, was the first person who understood Andersen's genius and who saw in his fairy tales the fruit of a unique imagination, his passport to immortality. Ørsted lived with his family in No.6, Studiestræde. The two men of genius were bound by mutual admiration throughout their lives.

"Thursday again at Mrs Bügel's, Friday with the Wulffs, where Weyse always comes on the same day and improvises."

C.E.F.Weyse was the famous composer who – at song master Siboni's house – had so sympathetically collected money for the poor boy at the later-so-memorable dinner party on 18th September, 1819. Captain P.Fr.Wulff was commander of the Royal Cadet Academy. In 1824, he was provided with an official residence in Frederik VIII's Mansion at Amalienborg. Wulff was famous as a translator

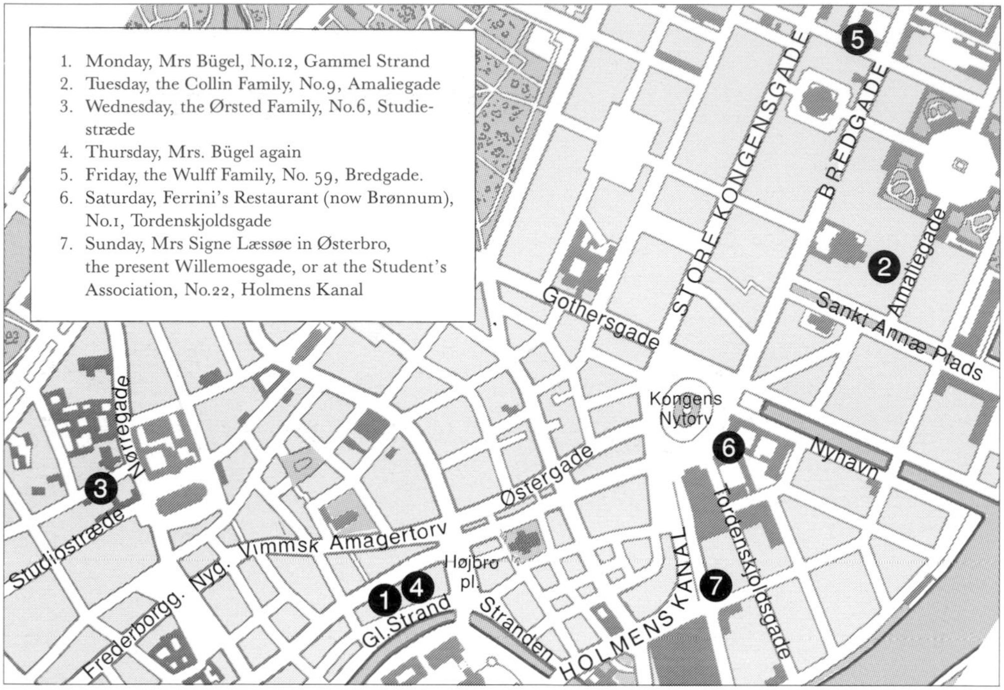

Andersen's Dinner Route

of Shakespeare and when, in 1821, the young Andersen had written a tragedy freely adapted from Shakespeare, he immediately rushed to Wulff's home to read it aloud to him. That was the start of a lifelong friendship with the whole family, and later we shall hear more of their hospitality towards this young man. They lived at that time in the present High Court building in Bredgade which, from 1827, was the school and living quarters of the naval cadets.

"Saturday is my free day. I eat wherever I am invited, otherwise at Ferrini's."

In 1838, the restaurant was in Kongens Nytorv between Charlottenborg and the Royal Theatre – the present Brønnum restaurant. If he was not feeling well, he would send out for food – mock-turtle as a rule.

"Sunday at Mrs Læssøe's, or at the Students' Association if I don't feel up to the long walk."

Mrs Signe Læssøe lived in what was at that time quite a rural district – in Østerbro just across from the lakes in the long white house, "Dalen", roughly where Willemoesgade is today. She was one of the motherly lady friends who early on believed in his literary talents. Faithfully and lovingly she shared in his tribulations and sympathised with his sensitive nature.

During Andersen's first year, the Students' Association was to be found on the corner of Boldhusgade and Admiralgade. There he had celebrated his very earliest triumphs as a reader. He was in frequent demand – also at the new address in Holmens Kanal where Hafnia now stands.

Not only did the maladroit bachelor never invite anyone to his home – or if he did, then for nothing more than coffee and cakes – not only that, but he himself never ate at home unless illness forced him to.

Restaurant *Brønnum*, No.1, Tordenskjoldsgade, was called Ferrini's in Andersen's day. Here the Poet often had his Saturday dinner. There has apparently been a demand for eating places in the close proximity of the Royal Theatre for 200 years.

Nyhavn Again

On 23rd October, 1871, Andersen writes in his diary, "At two o'clock drove to No.18, Nyhavn, my new address. Mrs Melchior accompanied me. The new rooms made a good impression."

One of the two rooms faced the yard, the other looked out onto Nyhavn. There the old poet often sat by the window observing life outside – as a surviving photograph testifies. There he would sit on the raised platform cutting silhouettes for his many friends, male and female. This was his address in Copenhagen until shortly before his death on 4th August, 1875. He now felt weak and decrepit. When he went out, he became short of breath and was afraid of slipping on the wet cobblestones or stumbling over the badly-laid paving.

But if he was physically debilitated, there was nothing wrong with his mind. In "New Fairy Tales and Stories", published around Christmas, 1871, his ironic showdown with benefactors and snobbery in "The Gardener and the Squire" is as effervescent as always. That too was read aloud to his circle of friends.

Right from the time the Poet was a child, he had loved to recite and read aloud. He had actually been teasingly called "The little reciter". Later he came to be highly regarded as a reader both in Copenhagen circles and at country mansions. He demanded full attention – whether he was reading to one listener or to more than one. When he read to the ladies of the house in No.18, Nyhavn, he demanded that they put down their needlework to listen.

A contemporary critic, Edvard Brandes, described his reading thus:

"Andersen's voice was deep, pure and flexible, was made more powerful or weaker with ease. His reading was not wholly dramatic, not like an actor's ... To hear him read 'The Ugly Duckling' – which enthusiastic audiences naturally often requested him to do – was not what is known as, to use a stupid word, an *experience* (because that is what most things in this world are). Rather it was an insight, revealed in glimpses, into what this rare and mistreated human soul had felt and suffered through in order to produce this little, immortal work of art ... He was a true man who had waged his war against all, and he seemed a considerable and original genius as he sat there in his chair, his wonderful head bowed over the book – the words of which he knew by heart."

A not uncritical observer of his recitations was song master Axel Grandjean, who notes in his memoirs:

"Andersen read his fairy tales quite humorously and when the tall, loose-limbed figure with the nervous twitches stood at the lectern, he could quite accurately mimic various animal voices and there was a becoming naivety about him. But a certain self-satisfaction showed through, and he was constantly on guard to see whether he was found funny enough, whereby some of the effect was lost."

No.18, Nyhavn is today owned by Denmark's National Bank. The Bank has generously made the apartments in the 200-year-old building available free of charge to visiting scholars from all over the world.

Andersen photographed by portrait-photographer Weller in his apartment in No.18, Nyhavn, 1873. This apartment, which was his final home (1871-75), was until recently occupied by an elderly artist who lived and breathed for the old Poet. He put his desk in the same place by the window and made paper cuttings with themes from the fairy tales. Apparently there is a spirit of inspiration in the rooms.

No. 67 Nyhavn. The Poet In Flesh And Blood

Walk down towards the harbour and cross left over the bridge to No. 67, Nyhavn. A commemorative plaque on the wall tells us that Hans Christian Andersen lived here from 1845-1864.

He had rented three rooms from sea captain Johannes Anholm for a monthly rent of 18 rixdollars. The poet did not have his own furniture, so what rough, simple furniture there was belonged to the Anholm family. The most respectable item was a mahogany sideboard with low side cupboards. On one of the cupboards was a bust of Jenny Lind, on the other a bust of Andersen himself made by Joseph Durham and which he had decorated with pink material. All these items are today to be found at the Hans Christian Andersen museum in Odense.

The Poet felt at home with the Anholm family, although he didn't like their dog - even though it was a large, good-natured creature. One of the daughters has told the story of how one day when Andersen appeared, the dog began to bark furiously. Andersen flew terrified up the stairs and, on reaching the safety of his own quarters, cried in his Funen accent, "Did it bite me? Did it bite me?"

Every day the Poet would put on his top hat and go to visit his friends, his latest work under his arm. One day when he came to visit the composer J.P.E. Hartmann, there was a wild commotion. One of their children had disappeared. On hearing this, Andersen at once volunteered to go and look for the child. Emma Hartmann looked at him and said, "Thank you, Andersen. What a good man you are! I shall go and see your play at the theatre this evening then, even though I have heard it is terrible."

His hearty manner was so endearing that people were put in a good mood just by meeting him in the street. The student actor Emanuel Hansen writes:

"I have never known anyone who could put so much into a greeting as he did when you met him in the street - especially at a slight distance - in Kongens Nytorv, for example, where he often walked from his lodgings in Nyhavn, along Charlottenborg to the Royal Theatre. If it so happened that he caught sight of me as I greeted him, it was not enough for him to raise his hat by way of answer; he would swing it out to one side in a merry gesture as far as his arm would reach, at the same time nodding to me with an expression so full of benevolence that it made me feel good for a long time afterwards."

He had now become so famous that admirers came from abroad to visit him. One of these visitors was John Ross Brown. He describes their meeting at the beginning of the 1860's as follows:

"Before me stood a tall, thin, loose-limbed, and bony figure, a man who was past his prime, but not yet old, with a pair of dancing eyes in a fine, wrinkled face that was mobile and alive. And in the middle of this face was a large, projecting nose which, by a whim of nature, was slightly crooked - and was flanked by two very prominent cheek bones below which were two large hollows. Countless wrinkles and furrows curved down around the corners of a large mouth, a wide, deep, irregular opening which might easily have resembled the jaws of some monster that would devour children - had it not been for the mild, sunny smile that played in the corners of the mouth and the compassion that shone forth from every fold and wrinkle.

"He took both my hands in his, clapped me heartily on the shoulder and bade me welcome, and immediately I knew that it was no other - could not possibly be any other - than the great Hans Christian Andersen."

Friendliness, compassion, life and warmth were the aura

No. 67, *Nyhavn* was the Poet's home from 1848 to 1865, and hence the place where he lived longest. Here he wrote *The Fairy Tale of My Life*. It is a beautiful house which, like so many others in the street, has undergone a thorough restoration. This side of the canal – with the odd-numbered houses – was always known as the "naughty side" because of the wild life that once flourished in the sailors' dives. Now it is fashionable to live on either side of the canal.

The house on the right, no. 69, bears the name *H.C. Andersen House - Nyhavn*. The 200-year-old house was inaugurated in 1991 in honour of the Poet. The permanent exhibition tells in sound and pictures the story of his life. In addition, however, the house embraces a creative cultural environment with changing thematic exhibitions, readings, lectures and musical entertainment.

From the café on the third floor there is a magnificent view of the canal and the harbour.

that emanated from Andersen. The early youthful pictures of him show that his eyes were unnaturally small, but by now they had opened. The overall impression was engaging, notwithstanding the large, powerful facial features. The world around him no longer thought of him as ugly and already he was virtually an historic figure! All the thoughts he had had and the feelings he had lived through illuminated his face from within with a soulfulness that one could not help but notice. He could see it himself and he became childishly happy when he saw a photograph taken in Munich by the photographer Hanfstängl: "Never have I seen such a beautiful and yet lifelike portrait of myself! I was thoroughly surprised, astonished, that the sunlight could make such a figure of beauty of my face. I am incredibly flattered, and yet it is but a photograph. You will see it, it is the only portrait that my vanity wishes to be handed on to posterity. How the young ladies will exclaim: To think that *he* never married."

Hans Christian Andersen looks quite satisfied with himself in this photograph taken by Hanfstängl in Munich 1860.

The Ugly Duckling Answers Back

From No.67, Nyhavn, we walk back in the direction of Kongens Nytorv to the corner of Bredgade and Store Strandstræde. Behind the corner house there was, in the old days, a house which came to be of enormous importance to Andersen – that of the Collin family. The front faced onto Bredgade while the building at the back faced towards Store Strandstræde.

After his first three years in Copenhagen, Andersen was in many respects a failure. He had been rejected as a dancer, a singer, and an actor, and the tragedy, "Alfsol", written in 1822, had been returned to him. There was one talent, however, which he possessed in abundance – he could make people take an interest in him. Jonas Collin, a member of the board of directors of the Royal Theatre and a financier, had read his "Alfsol" and recommended him to King Frederik VI, who financed his education during the following years. At the same time, the Collin family opened their doors to him, and he found there both parents and brothers and sisters.

"An awkward and clumsy half-timbered house lay situated here in this impressive street; an old-fashioned wooden balcony led up to the entrance on the first floor; the narrow, enclosed courtyard had a clumsy wooden gallery under the overhanging roof, but out towards the street itself an old lime tree spread its branches across the yard and up towards the pointed gable."

In other words, the Collin family lived on the first floor of "The Old House", as it was known, while on the ground floor there was a *conditori* which served chocolate and cakes and where half of Copenhagen met. Andersen too was a

The Collins' house seen from *Store Strandstræde,* later demolished.

Restaurant Els

regular customer. The bakers called him "The long, tall Sunday student".

The importance of the Collin family's home for the Poet cannot be exaggerated. But when you have a poet living under your roof, you run the risk of ending up in one of his works. The Collins did, indeed, appear – and not always in a flattering light! Their self-sufficient ways could drive him to despair, down-at-heel and eccentric as he looked for many years dressed in his ill-fitting clothes. Perhaps "The Ugly Duckling" may be read as the settling of an account between the ugly, impoverished budding poet and the self-sufficient family in Bredgade:

"'You don't understand me,' said the duckling. 'Well if we don't understand you, I should like to know who would! Surely you will never make out that you are wiser than the cat and the old woman – not to mention myself! Don't give yourself airs, child! Thank your Maker for all the kindness you have met with. Haven't you come to a warm room where you have company that can teach you something?'

"And the cat was master of the house, and the hen the mistress. And all the time they would say, 'We and the world' for they thought that they were half the world – and much the better half at that. The duckling thought there might be two opinions about that, but the hen would not hear of it."

In the fairy tale, "The Shadow", there is a bitter recollection of Edvard Collin, who was the same age as Andersen. Andersen had quite reasonably suggested that they should be on what in Danish corresponds to Christian-name terms (there are two forms of address in Danish – the formal, "polite" form *De*, and the informal, "friendly" form *du*), but Edvard had declined. This was turned into a bitter story about the arrogant shadow who refused to be on familiar terms with his master. The Poet has the last word after all. What was it that Strindberg said? "Take care, you devil, we shall meet in my next play!"

The Collin family moved from the house in 1838 and in 1845 sold it to pastry chef Grandjean – who demolished the dilapidated building and built a new house on the site. The popularity of the café continued for many years, and it became one of Andersen's regular haunts. The premises remain unaltered and now belong to Restaurant Els.

Further down Store Strandstræde, in No. 20, you will come to "Galerie Victoria", which is owned by the actor, Erwin Anton Svendsen. His highly unusual little shop is papered from floor to ceiling with old prints and lithographs. Below the ceiling are fixed layer upon layer of pictures, and in the window is a display of rare prints from Andersen's time with motifs from the theatre and Kongens Nytorv. If we trace Erwin Anton Svendsen's family tree back to around 1800, it turns out that he is the great-great-grandchild of Grandjean the pastry chef, who bought the Collin family's house. His great-grandfather was the Axel Grandjean who recorded his impressions of Andersen in his memoirs. A fairy tale can also reveal the connexions between people if we know how to turn the key.

The ground floor premises of *No. 3, Store Strandstræde*, were formerly the home of Grandjean's *conditori*. Andersen and Thorvaldsen were regular customers here. When Grandjean moved into his new house, Andersen honoured the *conditori* with a poem. Just as today's guests do in Restaurant Els, Andersen would sit and admire the six beautiful murals of female figures symbolising the four seasons plus the muses of dance and music. The murals were painted by Christian Hetch, one of the artists of that time with connexions to the Royal Theatre.

The Mad Dancer

We continue down Store Strandstræde to Sankt Annæ Plads, from where we can glance up to Bredgade. No.19 in those days was the home of Madam Schall, the dancer. She was the very first person the lanky boy from Odense visited in the hope that she might help him on in the world. Externally the house has changed a great deal, but the visitor can still see the stairs which Hans Christian climbed with trembling knees.

"Before I tugged the bell pull, I sank to my knees in front of the door and prayed to God that I might find help and protection here. At that moment, a maid servant with a basket on her arm came up the stairs. She smiled kindly at me, gave me a small coin and tripped off. I looked at her and the coin in astonishment. I was wearing my confirmation suit and must look very well-dressed, so I thought. How could she imagine that I wanted to beg. I called out to her. 'Oh, just keep it!' she called down to me and was gone.

"At length I was ushered in to the dancer, who looked and listened to me in great amazement ... In my own way I explained to her my burning desire to go on the stage. When she asked me what roles I thought I could perform, I told her one of the roles in "Cinderella". It had been performed by the royal players in Odense and the main role had so captivated me that I could play it by heart from beginning to end. I asked permission to remove my boots, as I was otherwise not light enough for the part, and now I took my big hat and used it as a tambourine and began to dance and sing:

'What do riches mean to me,
What is pomp and pageantry?'

"My strange gestures and my curious agility made the dancer think, as she herself has told me many times since then, that I was out of my mind, for which reason she got rid of me as quickly as possible."

One of the many addresses where Andersen resided was Sankt Annæ Plads No.22, on the ground floor. He lived in the house for only a few months in 1861.

We continue down Amaliegade. On the left, in No.9, Collin the elder lived from 1838. It is worth having a look in here and in No.11 seeing the half-timbered back houses which have just been restored. The wealth of detail in the windows, stairs, and oriels is a feast for the eyes.

The dancer
Anna Margrethe Schall
(1775-1852).

The Collins' House in *No. 9, Amaliegade*. Jonas Collin moved here in 1838. Now Amaliegade too became one of the Poet's regular eating places. His close ties to the Collin family are reflected in several fairy tales as well as in their voluminous correspondence. It is worth going in to look at the courtyard, which is rich in details from an architectural style now vanished.

On the opposite side, in No.10, was the famous Casino Theatre – now "Assurandørernes Hus" (The Federation of Danish Insurance Companies). In the theatre's 90-year history from 1847 to 1937 many festive performances were staged – among them "Around the World in 80 Days". Hans Christian Andersen's fairy-tale comedies, "Willie Winkie" and "Mother Elderberry" for example, also had highly successful runs here.

Continue now along Amaliegade to Amalienborg.

A Real Fairy Tale

To Hans Christian Andersen, 20 years old, aspiring poet and still a schoolboy under the eye of the formidable headmaster Meisling in Slagelse, the Christmas holiday of 1825 was particularly welcome. From his tiresome treadmill he was to be transported straight into a fairy tale. He was to live in the King's palace.

The Amalienborg mansion known as the Brockdorff Mansion – the one with the clock – was actually not yet a royal residence. It had long served as an academy for naval cadets. They lived on the upper floors while the officers occupied the rest of the mansion.

In 1824, the Shakespeare translator Captain P.Fr.Wulff had taken command of the academy and now lived in the mansion with his family. They were warm-hearted, hospitable people and, not least because of the children – Christian, Henriette, and Ida – their home became the centre of social life in Copenhagen. Andersen was received with open arms and was at once in good spirits:

"I have been given two rooms facing the square, one to sleep in, another with heating where I shall read in the morning. The ceiling arches high over my head so it is easy to imagine myself in a good knight's castle." But as usual he does not forget to thank the good Lord for his fantastic good fortune. His thoughts return to the first humble years in Copenhagen where he lived in poverty and misery. Now it is a different story to say the least!

"I was given by Wulff the three volumes of Skakspeare *(sic)* he has translated ... thousands of feelings flow through me. Oh what has God not done for me? It is like Aladdin at the end of the story when he looks out of the palace window and says, 'Down there I walked when I was a poor boy.'

"For 5 or 6 years I too walked down there, not knowing a soul in this town, and now I can hug myself, reading my Schekspear *(sic!)* up there in the house of a dear and respected family – oh God is good ... He has made me so happy."

Today the mansion is Queen Ingrid's private residence. The room where he read in the morning is now a large and cosily furnished bedroom, while the former bedroom serves as a dressing room. Before that it was Queen Margrethe's nursery.

The art historian Christian Elling has ingeniously worked out where it was that Andersen lived by studying contemporary drawings. With pride the Poet makes particular mention of the stately, square room with the four windows facing the palace square, and that one of his rooms was heated. Every day the servant came to make up the fire in the stove. Early one morning he awoke to an ice-cold room and tiptoed round in stockinged feet to find the servant, "But I got the wrong door and entered the maid's room. On discovering my mistake, I shot out." His rooms were situated in the "Southern Pavilion" in what is marked on the plan as the "Commander's Assembly Room for Officers". It is precisely in this pavilion – where the servants also lived and the back of which faces onto Toldbodgade – that the ceiling arches up in a beautiful, sweeping curve.

The young Andersen loved to live in his "dear palace". On 23rd December there was a ball in the banqueting hall. The king and the princes were present, the cadets in their fine uniforms. "The gilded rooms shone in the radiant gleam of the chandeliers." Andersen had also intended to dance, but at the sight of all this elegance he lost heart. Nor did he have anything to wear. "Oh if only I were more finely dressed."

He changed from his black jacket to a grey dress coat, "But everyone was black, I was only grey. So I could

Amalienborg, Frederik VIII's Mansion. It was on the top floor of the pavilion to the right of the equestrian statue that Andersen stayed for Christmas 1825. The palace, designed by architect Nicolai Eigtved and built around 1750 during the heyday of Rococo, is considered one of northern Europe's finest buildings. The statue of Frederik V is a masterpiece created by the French sculptor, Jacques Saly, and was presented to the people of Copenhagen in 1771.

neither stand nor walk away. Ølenslæger talked to me, I felt embarrassed. They probably think I am a waiter." In despair he flew into his room, cursing the fate which had not provided him with suitable clothes. Then, however, he regained his composure, for he had something which the others did not – ideas! And, "While the carriages rolled outside and the ideas rolled inside my head, I fell asleep."

Shortly afterwards the mansion was taken over by the royal family. In May, 1826, the king's daughter, Vilhelmine Marie became engaged to Prince Frederik (later Frederik VII), and what could be more suitable as a royal residence? The Naval Academy vacated the premises on 1st April, 1827, and it was architecht to the court, Jørgen Hansen Koch, who was entrusted the task of converting the mansion. He fell in love with Wulff's daughter, Ida, and when they were married, a new hospitable home opened its doors to the Poet.

Frederik and Vilhelmine's marriage was a disappointment. They were divorced in 1838. In 1869, it became Frederik VIII's residence and has borne his name ever since.

A new epoch in the history of the mansion was heralded when, in 1935, Crown Prince Frederik married the Swedish Princess Ingrid. They immediately set about removing all the Victorian trappings and renovating the mansion so that it met with the demands of a modern royal couple for a beautiful, distinguished, and comfortable home.

Since the death of Frederik IX, it has been, as mentioned earlier, Queen Ingrid's home. With her extensive knowledge of the history of the mansion, she has made a thorough study of how it once looked and has restored as much as possible to its original state.

Queen Ingrid's bedroom in the Frederik VIII mansion.

The Changing of the Guard, at 12 o'clock on a winter's day, as seen from Andersen's former reading room.

The Magic Galoshes

During the period 1783-1916, Nos.23-25, Amaliegade were the home of the Royal Maternity Hospital. The garden which belongs to the beautiful old building is the largest in town. It is open to the public during normal hours, so you can go in and see the 200-year-old pear tree in the middle.

The ordinary hospital ward was situated in the part of the building which today houses the Museum of Applied Art. This is where a part of the story of "The Magic Galoshes" takes place. These galoshes have the power to fulfil all the wishes of anyone wearing them. This, however, is a secret, so the galoshes come to inflict bad luck wherever they go.

Then as now, there are tall railings around the building, both in Amaliegade and in Bredgade. In Andersen's story, a young medical student who is on duty at the hospital has an irresistible urge to pop out, just for a quarter of an hour. He has heard that, "Very thin medical students have been able to squeeze through the railings and thus make their short, clandestine calls." The student is wearing the galoshes, it is raining, and, unfortunately, he happens to wish that he could put his head outside the railings - just his head! Immediately he is trapped. Since he can neither get his body through, nor his head back, he remains stuck until, just by chance, he happens to wish that he were free again.

At No.31, Amaliegade, there is a wide alley leading to Bredgade. Have a look at the Museum of Applied Art's beautiful courtyard in No.68, Bredgade, before continuing down to the end. Turn left along Esplanaden to get to the lilliput town of Nyboder. Alternatively, you can continue straight on to Kastellet.

For 350 years, the houses of Nyboder have been let to naval crews and workers from the naval dockyards. Over

The garden, *No. 23, Amaliegade*. In former times all the houses in the Amalienborg area had such a garden, but the price of land is too expensive for that today. The garden is open to the public during normal office hours.

The railings around the *Museum of Applied Art* are the same as in Andersen's time. It was between these railings that the medical student in *The Magic Galoshes* got his head stuck.

the centuries, Nyboder and its "old guard" have become national symbols. For the first couple of hundred years Nyboder was regarded by the more respectable classes as a wretched working-class district. But gradually Nyboder became an idyll and was idealised by several poets. Hans Christian Andersen too felt such an attraction to Nyboder that he wrote about it in his fairy tale, "Mother Elderberry".

"In Nyboder there grew a large flowering tree. It grew in the corner of a humble, little backyard. Under the tree, two old people sat one afternoon in the most beautiful sunshine. It was an old, old sailor and his old, old wife."

Up in the tree lives Mother Elderberry, the very symbol of reminiscence. While the old couple sit under the fragrant elder blossoms, she makes sure that their whole life unfolds before them.

Nyboder was built by Christian IV around 1630 for Navy personnel. The long yellow buildings were originally single-storey houses. Behind the blocks there are small, idyllic backyards which, now as then, help to make the area an attractive place to live in. It was in one of these backyards that the Poet saw *Mother Elderberry*. The buildings, with their fine constructional details, are architectural gems.

Kastellet

To get to Kastellet, walk across the moat and through the King's Gate. As early as during the reign of Christian IV, the corner facing out towards the Sound had been fortified with fieldworks. But it was not until after the Swedish siege of Copenhagen in 1658-59 that Kastellet acquired its star-shaped fortifications. In 1663-64, the garrison was quartered in the long barrack buildings which since then have housed many different regiments.

When you stand on the ramparts looking out over the town, it is difficult to imagine how detached and idyllic these fortifications were in Hans Christian Andersen's time. In those days they marked the extremity of a whole long line of ramparts encircling Copenhagen from Tivoli, along the present Vestervold, to Nørrevold and Østervoldgade.

Through the two peepholes in the wall to the right of the window the prisoners in the adjoining prison could follow the service.

The long barracks are built parallel to and in continuation of one another. The place has not always been so idyllic – far from it! For many years there was a gaol in the Stjernestok building, and in 1725 a prison for State prisoners was built on to the church. In their cold cells the prisoners could thus hear the minister preach his sermon, the organ play, and the congregation sing their hymns.

"It is autumn, we stand on the Kastellet ramparts and look out over the sea at the many ships and at the Swedish coast which rises up in the evening sun. Behind us the ramparts drop sharply. There are fine trees, the yellow foliage falls from the branches. Down there are dismal houses and inside where the sentry goes his rounds it is cramped and forbidding. But it is even darker behind the barred hole where captured slaves sit, the worst criminals ..."

Both the ground-floor and the first-floor cells have been preserved. In the walls adjacent to the church, the slanting peepholes can still be seen through which the prisoners could watch the service. Both the church and the prison were restored in 1987, while the barrack buildings were repainted in their original red colour back in the 1970's.

Kastellet's Prison has been built onto the church. The cells are still preserved from the time this was a state prison, and many famous prisoners of the state were kept here. The romantic mixture – both idyllic and grim – inspired Andersen to write the story, *From the Ramparts of the Citadel*. The long barracks are named after the military units that lived here. Nowadays it is the Life Guards who stand guard at Kastellet.

The Little Mermaid

Continue now through the Norwegian Gate at the north end of the barracks and down to the harbour. There at the water's edge, still on military ground, sits The Little Mermaid, one of Hans Christian Andersen's many famous fairy tale characters. She has become the symbol of the city of Copenhagen and a "must" for every tourist. She is not an imposing monument, sitting there with her fish tail. But in her graceful form there is a tiny glimpse of the fairy-tale world that the Poet has given to us.

But for our Poet and writer of fairy tales this little bronze figure would never have existed. "The Little Mermaid" is the unhappy love story of a mermaid who falls hopelessly in love with a handsome earthly prince. From this moment on she wishes only to live in the world of people and to gain an immortal soul. Mermaids become the foam on the ocean when they die.

And so she goes to the sea witch - who gives her a potion which turns her fish's tail into a pair of legs. The object of her longing - to live at the prince's court - is thus fulfilled. On the other hand, her life is now filled with suffering. Not only does every step she takes feel like treading on sharp knives, she has also lost her beautiful voice - that the witch took in payment.

The condition for gaining an immortal soul is the prince's love. But although the prince is extremely fond of the little mermaid, nevertheless he falls in love with another. On his wedding night she learns that she can save herself by killing him. But she chooses death for herself.

This, by Andersen's own account, was the only one of his works which he himself felt moved by when he wrote it.

The Little Mermaid is one of Andersen's most beautiful and most touching fairy tales. She is also Copenhagen's most popular tourist attraction. Sculptor Edvard Eriksen's work was erected here in 1913. A bridal couple and their happy wedding guests just happen to sail past – the bride in white, the groom in uniform. A fairy tale lives on.

Works by Hans Christian Andersen mentioned in the text

Hans Christian Andersen became a swan even though Copenhagen was a duckyard where the ducks pecked at him. Might it not have been this lack of recognition which urged the Poet to excel? Could this be *The Ugly Duckling*, now transformed into a swan, in the moat at Rosenborg?

1	The King's Garden	Rosenborg
2	Frederiksberg Hill	Roskildevej
3	Rahbeks Alle 23	The Hill House
4	The Town Hall Square	Hans Andersens statue
5	Tivoli	
6	No.27 Farvergade	Vartov
7	No.18 Vestergade	The Guards' Inn
8	Nytorv	The Courthouse
9	Slutterigade	The Jailhouse
10	Nørregade	Copenhagen Cathedral
11	Købmagergade	The Round Tower. Trinitatis Church
12	Gråbrødretorv	
13	No. 9Valkendorfsgade	The Danish Post and Telegraph Museum
14	Nos.5-7 Købmagergade	Erik Bering's Flowers
15	No.6 Amagertorv	Royal Copenhagen
16	Christiansborg Riding-Ground	Court Theatre – The Theatre Museum
17	No.2 Posthusgade	Thorvaldsen's Museum
18	No.21 Højbro Plads	Dorothea and Moritz Melchior
19	No.18 Ved Stranden	Den gyldne Fortun, Riborg Voigt and Jenny Lind
20	No.20 Dybensgade	Where Andersen lived 1820-22
21	No.6 Vingårdsstræde	Where Andersen lived 1827-28
22	No.13 Kongens Nytorv	Hotel du Nord, now Magasin du Nord. – where Andersen lived 1838-47
23	No.17 Kongens Nytorv	à Porta, restaurant. Where Andersen lived 1866-69
24	No.19 Kongens Nytorv	Hviids Vinstue, pub
25	No.34 Kongens Nytorv	Hotel d'Angleterre, where Andersen stayed on a number of occasions
26	Kongens Nytorv	The Royal Theatre
27	No.1 Tordenskjoldsgade	Brønnum, restaurant, formerly Ferrini
28	No.17 Tordenskjoldsgade	Andersen's home 1870-71
29	Kongens Nytorv	Charlottenborg. Sculptors' Garden
30	No.18 Nyhavn	Andersen's home 1871-75
31	No.20 Nyhavn	Andersen's home 1834-38
32	No.67 Nyhavn	Andersen's home 1848-65
	No.69 Nyhavn	H.C.Andersen · Nyhavn
33	No.3 Store Strandstræde	Els (restaurant, formerly Grandjean's Conditori
34	No.20 Store Strandstræde	Galerie Victoria
35	No.22 Sankt Annæ Plads	Andersen's home some months 1861
36	No.9 Amaliegade	Jonas Collin's home
37	Amalienborg	P.Fr.Wulff and family
38	Nos.23-25 Amaliegade	The original Garden of the Maternity Hospital
39	Nos.29-31 Amaliegade	Museum of Applied Art, formerly Frederik's Hospital
40	Nyboder	
41	Kastellet	Church and prison
42	Langelinie	The Little Mermaid